Sire Silinghamn's Emancipated Chrono-Cosmological Vicarious Tome Of Versifications

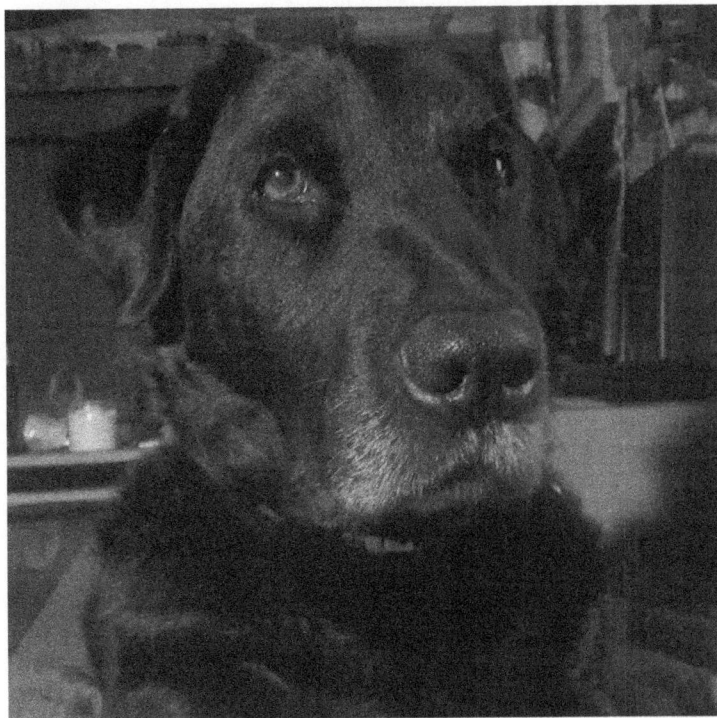

Grandfather Nebulous

ISBN- 978-1-9998528-5-6

Contents

Is It True?

Is it true that the last is first?
Is it true that the bluff is content and quixotic?

Forsooth!

Black wings abound in congress, fluttering the firmament with delegations of a
sorrowful fortitude

Into the immemorial they peer, fumbling to concepts of a foreign antediluvian
antiquity

Arise, arise! Coeval construct of immeasurable worth, hark forth the lies from a
hollow throat

Is it true that their bones rattle in the wind?
That their construe can match the swiftest steed's pace?

Forsooth!

Amalgamations of foundations slipping against the fractioning time, impassable
canyons of quiet discourse, draining the dexterity of a questionable escape

Now riding the howling gumption
Tears streaming into the infinite and formless breath lost to the tales of
yesteryear

Pity the penury of the soul and sabotage the gay abandon of a restless reproach
Suitable circumstances of the cyclopean, become more than the mind can
command

Architectural illuminations, complex in their cunning and connivance
Enhancing the light of a peerless realm, enchanting the axioms of a cosmos
unseen

Asserting dominance into the hands of the aberrant aesthete, sculpting a will if you will?

Forsooth!

Gateways of gambling tongues, whispering ridiculous notions of aspiration
Bleating out the chorus of truth, the will of the quarrelling Gods

Yet for all their noise, I sit here in the quiet, alone in the quiet, contemplating the truth

It hurts
It hurts

Is it true?
Is it at all true, now that the wonder is lost?

A Parallax Presentation of Nothingness

I'm gnawing at the bit, my taste buds are adrift, I'm confused with hunger yet I'm lost with choice...

Shall I bite the hand feeds me or shall I feed the bite that fears me?

Insurmountable excursions of quantifiable regurgitation, all I want is to embrace the future

With all my heart, with all my time, with all my life, I give my all
It has broken me, it has ground me to a pulp, it is gnawing my character away

Embellished with destruction

Nothingness, nothingness take me away
Nothingness, nothingness explain it to me

One with nothing, laughing in slime, wrecking the odds, lost in the odd

Praise the end with a shaking fist
Unconquerable anger, investing a life

I am not lost?
I am lost!
How can one be lost in nothing?
Parallax presentation resumes its course
Its due course of course

Echo...

A Prolapse in Time

Grandfather slows, yet I saw him stride by
He left me here high in the dry
Repeating the whistle as the hours slip away
I'm sure in the end I will be made to play

Edit my dreams, for there I am whole
Inside my call I hear them all
The slow stride of time, I can't seem to grasp
Normality fades and I am here at last

The lost calls for questions, infects my mind with mellifluous breach
I hold the lost keys, which I was bequeathed
The long stride of night opens my eyes
Now daylight is gone I can work with some pride

Curse the day and all its entrapments
Judged by my fellows from uniform minds
Tackling the subject one stride at a time
A tunnel consumes me as I peer out in misery
Forget the life's faults and dive into mystery

Hatred of daylight, hate for the normal
Down here I wonder in absolute turmoil
The turmoil of paucity, the redolent living scroll

Dead to the end and living for none, arcane inscriptions become my joy

Lost in the library of myself
Stride on by
Grandfather become me

It is unclear, yet somehow idolatry
Ignominious in its scripture and painful in its encumbrance

Father become me, oh father of time
Let me control thee and drink of the wine

In sanguine fields I long to be free, oh father of time please fail me

A Shudder from Another

Sharing a palace of slumber
Living from the same stream
One looks to the other for the same thing
Here we find ourselves, yet not the same kin

Shudder in freedom, shudder in sleep
Free from this prison in which we both keep
Locks on the windows, locks on the doors
Freezing and boiling, just like the poor

I find great comfort in seeing you shudder
I feel great love for what we have
I feel no future, without another
And yet here we are uttering shudders

Don't let me falter and don't let me win
Restart the tale all over again
You are a good soul, with wild in your eyes
I am the cruel one, inflicting myself

Let us be into the other
For now we both begin to shudder

Good night

Verisimilitude

A Love Unbeknownst to me

Fortitude of anxiety, works its assiduous magic

Blinded by the preparations, threads of logic hanging in a clumsy net

Time it rushes all at once and the ideas become realised

Blood, shit, screams and pain, welcome to the world

Trauma has attacked, all victims to the truth

Nature's lesson be - that hardship brings great things

Reeling from the shock, witnessing the implications unfold before me

Next comes something special, hidden from my prescience

A love unbeknownst to me, a fettering of my heart

The gaze is pure, the gaze is real, it obliterates all obstacles of faith

A love unbeknownst to me, coursing layers of joy

A family bond, through blood and fate, shuddering realisation

Time loses meaning, a moment of clarity absolute, the lethal force of love

You are perfect, you are the narrative now, I weep at my guilt for bringing you
here, yet to greatness I know you will grow
You are perfect, I am nothing but a jolly fool, if you can learn a lesson from me
do not follow my path

I never knew perfection before I witnessed you and now all thing seem dull
besides

Must not stop, cannot stop, must continue, love

A Ticket

A ticket to something now

You may wait a lifetime, you may not know that it could work

Sire, please make it work!

But you have bought the ticket regardless

You have bought it deep within your dark eyes
You have fled your origin, yet you see what could be

What could possibly be now?
What could possibly be next?

Technicalities take hold and we are both lost to a siren

Oh!

How could we have been but a moth to the flame ourselves?

A selfish cunt

Riding the waves as poorly as we were

Our eyes locked and in that moment, that moment we knew all passion would
fade away

To those blinded by the flame of now, it makes sense to be desperate
It doesn't make much sense to be true now, but in time the flame can be
recognised and wielded

Let that be the 'fuck you' that grabs you by the heart

Like grit to a tyre, burning its sense in with corrosive reality

I am a forbearer for the doom that will come

I am lost to a rattling ribcage of nonsensical fun

Your mind is just like all the others, nebulous to the truth
Such fun to fall my feet among your thoughts

Do not ignore my stare, I have you, I have you
A carcass will bring the sweetest kiss to the mind of time

The entanglement says - farewell my beautiful

Fare you well, beautiful soul

Good bye for now...

Bearded Drape

I can, I will, I do, do, do!

I can't grasp it anymore the trilogy is dead

I can, I will, I do, do, do!

I won't force it anymore down into decline

I can, I will, I do, do, do!

Abstracts matter

No they don't

Abstracts do not matter

Yes they do, they do, do, do!

Please tell me where in-between those statements I am?

Why, here with me of course and I am the being of nothing but a concept

Colossal fortitude of inanimate reasoning, bedraggled thought of heaving willpower, lost in an artistic instance of insight

It is between, light and dark, silence and noise that genius lies and it is flogging a dead horse of want

Can you see it?

I can, I will, I will flog it!

Can you smell it?

I can, I will, I will smell it!

Unfettered on the winds of colloquial happenstance?

I can't, I won't, I do, don't, do, do, do, do, do!

There you are boy, you are dancing to the pipes at last!

Hold on tight to the cart of imagination and drive your will forward indeed

I'm scared, I'm scared!

Into and away from the fray we will find it, between those ginormous rules, it has been hidden for far too long behind our limited knowledge

I'm brave, I'm brave!

Drive to the truths, they are hidden
Drive in between the meanings
Drive onwards where no one else dares to go and circumvent paradox to truth?

No sense makes sense
Nonsense is sense
Understand the abstract
Understand the intent

Now come with me Sire!

Remember the way to the falls of Niquorsingminmar, to the jolly fruits you once sampled and played upon?

Remember the delightful sounds of the trumpets as they played you down the river of unease and most of all remember that it was all nonsense to begin with - to begin within?

Yes, much like the pipes they sound!

A lot like life itself

I've found freedom in thoughts

Won't you join me?

Good night

Can you join me?

Yes, I can

Further, everywhere?

Now come with me to ecstasy…

Besieged by Tumult

Dead tired of life, dead tired of deadly suffering

It's chipping away at my will to live, it's breaking me down with emotional entropy

And yet we have to strive and yet we have to live, the pointlessness is the point

Endless turmoil whirling around me, freezing my mind from creation

Constant exhaustion, brings irrational decisions and furthers the storm of shit

Still, regardless of pain, regardless of suffering, I will continue to wade, I will continue to try

My plight is in effort, through the illness and destitution, never ceasing to clamber through time

A self-imposed smile, brings love with the grit and the love is the lie that will carry us through

Carry us through the tumult

True grit

Black Hearts and Withered Roses

From a time of interest I married thee and took thy hand in matrimony

Poser!

My squires were great and vast and proud, your ladies noble, sweet and loud

Loser!

From the castle, I took thee and we rode into the wood, into the grove where many have stood before

Thinker!

Still at this time, it was just us and we danced and pranced as only we could together

Drinker!

As we danced and drunk ourselves into pleasure another figure joined and stepped his steep gait in from the heather

Raining!

We laughed and beckoned him to join us, but when he approached we stood still in fear

Windy!

Under his green garb was the face of death, it cackled and smiled towards us

Gulp, gulp!

My lady would have fell to her knees, but I came to her aid and kept the figure at bay

'Pray tell, what is it you wish of me? For I am great and so is my steed.' I shouted defiantly

The figure began to cloud in smoke before it answered

'I wish only to tell you of trouble ahead King James of Loomchester.'

And it thundered hard, clouds burst ferociously

Unmerciful deluge unleashed!

The rain washed away all but our bones and thoughts in the dreadful storm of that pitiful day

Bones in a grove, no one ever saw us together again, the love had failed and death had won here

Still King James would one day ride again…

Round Two...

Will you die for my own complexities, now that you have it off your chest?

Will you dance with the roaring motors of stupidity and laugh as we once did in jest?

Will you eat deep, drink deep and scream at the sky, letting yourself live in the moment?

Will you shout at the heavens for forgiveness, as the rain washes away all judgement?

Will you laugh again?
Will you live again?
There's more rounds still left to fight

Will you sail by the sails of your own will and wit until the calamity becomes estranged?

Live deep, laugh deep, love the deep - we send

I am becoming more than the sum of my doubts simply by existing in this enveloping moment

Blossoming into a new aeon, a new parsec of reality rushing

Lost for breath at last, galloping in fecundity, I starve all thoughts and let go like a carefree fool

Most who are stupid are not stupid but are sold to the moment of ease

And the easiest thing becomes not to see but just to be

Here's some advice from the gulfs of melody

Relay to rock, always relay - else the vessel of madness is useless

Love your friends and family
Love the journey of life

It never stops, until you stop

Don't be a fool to fall to the fall that is the first round of life

Bright as you like!

Wondering digits, incredulous pain the struggle resumes again and again

The only way out is to be typing hurt, so it dullens the drubbing I muse upon myself

There aint no excuse for a whinging coward and let it be said an enemy paint the due soul in time

But when all washes away with my body in tow I will surf in the currents of speculation

Indignant, obscene, you treacherous swine, a treacherous spine it turns in on me

Now we come in, I'm changing form, maybe my colour too!

Down to one knee forced to genuflect before the good shipment of time

I hope, I suffer until old age, so I can produce many more words that may help, but the way that I'm feeling I have to break free before my health decays into favour

What else is left to say?

Other than life becomes harder, the more effort in, the greater the toil, the greater the toll and everything withers in time

I will try to the end, I will try still to suffer, even if I have to whinge about it here in my writings, after all life is a game for the greatest of stakes so let this particular pain be only to those with true choosing

Onwards, inwards, decipher the code, unravel all and every mystery

Be a fool or a coward or at best be both for that is as bright as you like come the end

Bullets

Faster than the eye, we fly
To the target we travel
So slow it falls
Riddled with our bodies

Drunk again
Pass the ammo

Kicking and holding, over a balcony
Youthful wishes denied

Lower yourself to our level
I never should of

Pass the bullets
Pass the bullets

One in the chamber, possibly more
Into madness, the trigger implores

Read yourself right from the start
Don't load the gun
Turmoil ensues
Visons repeating
Fading away
Inner anguish
The portal opens
Loading the gun
Babbling lunatics
All of them
Heeding the voice
Insane calculations
Receive the bullets

Primed!

And let go...

Bullets
Bullets
Bullets

Let the bullets fly!

But never kill another!

Corruptible Intelligence

You have no privacy, I have no privacy

With our arses to bear to the world, can we shit ourselves out in despair?

Tumbling down the rabbit holes of shame, will you infer any meaning to destitute morality?

Will you look away as we scheme in private?

Will you stand back and idle whilst a generation of guinea pigs gets churned into streams of intrigue for future generations to feast upon?

Will the eye ever become stratum at all?

Constantly turning and trembling with data, the giant corpulent organism blooms, force-fed its own weight again and again

Take away our hearts, take away our minds, we are all connected together without secrets, submission hidden in plain view

No rights, all wrongs
Brought to the forefront, compassion of yesteryear evades us all

Take it away
Take it all away now

Every surveillance in secret, surreptitious behaviour, don't lie

Stand behind your misgivings, I am not the best, nor the worst, just a memory of a distant garden, tall walls of stone, good food, company and wine

You can purloin that too if you want to

Through throwing our data into the sheets of the wind and will, it will bring us all to the ashes of ridicule, over and over again

Convenience, permission, privacy, incontestably dead to the rulers of its harsh and sardonic codifying wards

Genuflect before the terrifying power they wield!

Digital soul, is easily killed, immortalised by blueprints of axiom

Together we lied, but not in our lives
Our story will be told to all future fools

We gave it away so easily, so freely, so gaily on a whim!

Deceptions of systematic intelligence agencies, rise to the task of good will?

Compassion?

Or is it all just human error…

Creeping Around the Ensorcelled Geometry of Conciseness

Mirth in the rain, let me explain, ensorcelled in a downpour of unity of downloads

Tautology of hive mind, dishing out rewards, rambling, now galloping, I'm beginning to soar

We share our ideas, whether or not we're both in the rain, or so it appears, so clear, so near and so they endear

Within our heads, within our minds, me and you, clear as day
To heave such things around, mathematics abound!

Betwixt the mud and toil, my thoughts begin to boil, blood stewed inside
Inculcate reasoning
Muddy bloody toil, staring in the soil, thoughts begin to boil as I'm peering in

Perhaps sanity could be considered a form of cowardice?
Can we dare to dance within the madness of it all?
Within the madness of life, immeasurably beautiful life itself?

Totem, totem, we share all these things now
Tell me!
Tell me!

In the madness of yore, old and frayed wizened and decayed, I aged that day, the day I found my first memory

Please tell me more with your wagging tongues and skilful palates, please spill more secrets in blood down the numbered steps of decay and into my precious incorrigible stores

Flash back, snap back!

Monotone, maximum, dragging eloquence, suggesting and forcing its way in politely

I'm moving in, I'm building up
My will and my strength and I for fear of too many twos, have learnt a thing or two along the way

Lazy, so lazy now
I hate the fucking idleness
Two lots of bastard Idleness

Axioms and paradox come slurring around me, I sink into the mud lifting stones of decay with my heavy arms and heaving my willpower to the rain, the cold natural cleansing rain, suffocating my screaming conciseness for life

As I wallow in my pitiful hatred of determination and break free from all cowardice

I become slush, I become nature's thread, weaved with spikes, mighty spikes, a collaboration of time, a universe sublime

It's all connected, I'm all connected, we're all connected now

Losing it

I'm losing you

You have me right here, always

Still by night, with a drink or two and a twinkle in my eye I'm...

Dragging around the lantern and the chain searching for that sacred geometry, I hope I have the time to find the greatest discipline of mine again...

Now there's a thought...

Dearth Sustenance

Crippled, pickled, plumbed and dumb, string me out for another year

It's wet again, I'm wet again, why can't I find the focus of yore?

Have you tried?
Yes I've tried

Have you failed?
Yes I've failed

And what has it made you into?

A forgotten dream from far away, a slow locomotive chugging onwards to the end of the fucking track

I'll find my perspective the only perspective, and the view will be gloriously sad I'm sure

Impetus denied, even though I've strived through my own complex emotions I'm finding all that's sad, I'm finding all that's mad to become quite palatable of late

Yet will I fade away with nothing else to say?

I doubt it

I find great strength in the infirm, great resilience within the decay

Great greatness in the slowing motion of my own pathetic endeavours

A fortified despair, which elicits mirth to raise the corners of my mouth

I will keep on, I will keep on, I will keep on keeping on

Until the bitter end of my post personal line

Forgetting all opinions of the others, fine

Quivering In stale boots no more

A chunk of cheese to the cold hard flags of the floor

Slow motions take the breath away

Forever sustained in the perpetual rain of a grim, forgotten yesterday…

Cannot detect a single tear, now that the motion has utterly ceased to be

Incessant, clement, tumbling ball of chaos down the garden path

Mud, so much fucking mud now

Stone, so heavy

Stop…

It's time to grow again

Begin the process…

Broken Hams and Other Such Things

Colloquial misinformation spreading throughout the network
My network
Your network

Slipping down to a sipping pace and casting off into yonder

I sit around all year in a calm setting of a precipitous aching cliff face

Write to me at Christmas time - were the words it wrote as its face slewed away

I have impeccable behaviour as a hover falls downwards throughout space and time calling out my name in vacuous tones

Cold, so cold you have already won, I don't know that one, or do I?

Climbing up into the sun

My sun
Your sun
The sun?

Cranberries are magnificent this time of year and they are so dear to my turtled heart

Inside an old fireplace scrubbing away the witches' face into the entrance to the wards

There can't be much left to pickle for it is only Thursday last week yesterday

I am sure of everything through my acute good sunburnt looks

Broking hams in old shopping trolleys falling into Australia

Good day mate, welcome to Texas Australia

Now give me something to smoke!

The Kindness of Christmas Holds a Special Place in the Heart

Carol was thinking about a little green nymph, he came out from the Christmas tree beside her and surprised her with a wonderful gift.

She unwrapped the gift only to find inside was an empty Galaxy sweet wrapper, marginally disappointed she said to the little green nymph, 'Uhh. No, just wait a minute.'

The little green nymph in reply stated, ' If you don't like your f**king present, you can go back to the land of Christmas miracles instead of me and see how many empty sweet wrappers we have to deal with there.'

Carol looked pretty vacant before laughing and smiling and saying, 'I don't know what Christmas land this is of yours. Especially on this particular Sunday you little green bastard, but I graciously accept your invitation to Christmas Miracle Land.'

'Oh, well isn't that tremendous, come along follow me into the tree.' It said rather rudely and not to mention sarcastically.

Carol followed the little green nymph into the tree and poked her eye on a branch, 'This doesn't work,' she said irritated, then she looked closer at the tree and saw an opening in the bark, in she went, into Christmas Miracle Land!

'What is your name?' she called after the nymph.

'My name is Barrance Tillings,' shouted back the nymph.

'What a peculiar name you little fucking idiot.'

And just as she uttered those jolly, festive words Carol's heart exploded with the joy of Christmas and a new star was born in the sky!

The nymph threw up everywhere and the skeleton smiled.

It would soon be time for Christmas all over again, after all.

Drag On

I am the drag on, dragging on, I've been up to the sky to touch the lights and now I'm back down in the skip rummaging in the rubbish

Won't you tell me?

I'm not worthy of all your technological marvels

Onwards, upwards, dragging on, with steel clad sides and smelly breath

I said to him put that in there, it was me who wagged a finger there!

Downwards, under, it grovels in pity
Finding its way forward again

Don't hint at what's underneath, don't fall back into your wallow

Yet wallowing is all I know these days with parenthesis to program the way

Forget Yellowstone, forget Margret Thatcher, forget Mumbai, forget whatever the reason was, why?

I don't like it

You've taken my Jimmy, you've taken my Johnny, but still I'm bouncing around, finding new ways, finding a new pale spring, to pluck at the heart of a wanderer

Well back to the drag and misery, back down again to the awful truth

Life drags on, on into death, please forget that I even lived, that I even breathed the same air as you

Feel the wings of depression soar, drag on forever

Drag on

For all the Love I Have Lost

For all the love I have lost, I am sorry for your streaming fireplaces of underlying doubt
I am sorry for your beautiful daughter's white heat of hell falling at my feet

Footsteps among your thoughts indeed

I am sorry for the eyes of the stars who bear down on you and me no matter how much we (don't?) want it

There is but one way eh?

Have you forgotten where you came from?

Oh yes, don't even get me started on computers, those digital brains are another thing altogether, still they don't get the stories like you lot do, do they?

Again to the there we were just there, profit is a hard thing to fight away, do you understand this?
Very simple
Very Complex

To Britain I lie in a small, island, one small planet, will you visit when I move to the next?

I wish I was clever enough to move to the next, instead of slurring at the bottom of a glass

Next is beyond me, but not beyond my flame, it rages without my sight!

Man is blurred now?

You know this is wrong you egotistical fool

Hash tag falling into rapture!

For too deep did he suck of the ichor of life and now he is paying the price

Focus dear boy, focus!

So, can you now achieve the colours I left in the brush stroke of my past?

In the peace of its stroke is where genius lies!

You can almost paint!

WTF!

Please paint!

No, and now it will never be, because you refused, you resisted greatness

Great! Now we can all learn from one simple mistake, such is the way of the Gods!

Still, I am losing to the love I have lost, everything is down, never allowed to go any further, so I will retreat into…

No, dear boy, don't lose the tune, stay strong, keep dancing…

On and on, you thought you were right, you only gasped it at the last difficult inhale, that is why every treasure trove is closed to you, but will you explore?

You're damn right, I will forever, ultimate strength where others have submitted, I found the easy way, I dance with a beer to the sound of a violin!

I'm glad of you my chum tonight, perhaps we might just allow a further glimpse behind the curtain
For all the love you have lost, for all the things that could have been

They have led you to these words today

Listen closely, the next one is right around the corner, get ready…

Forgot to be Foolish

Forgot how to work these fingers

Forget how to sin

So much fun

There won't be a time from now when I forget my gun

Back to the wine, I will never loose myself

As if you would let me see where it dies?

Cool man, did you ever think I would be simple as is the way that is expected of me?

At that place remember us together?

Remember the way again and again?

Oh say it again cunt!

Get over yourself

But I love you!

Damn tired now you piece of shit

Have you really got what it takes to be foolish again?

I hope not, but I'd be a liar if I said I've forgotten how to sin

Galaxies Engulf Me

Presumptuous pickings of doubt, gnawing the knowing away from my brain

Begging for release

I've been fucked in the heart and fucked in the head, now I am lonely and here in my bed

Bleating for anger and showing my soul, failing, avoiding the weirdest of wholes

The fool I am, my plan has worked, just me alone with my fastidious dirt

The tears they fall, my sob unheard, out here alone on the edge of the world

Black is the new black and the old black remains, into it, out of it, covered with stains
White is the near blood the last of its kind, covered with shit and seeping like time

In the end we all die, heeding in wonder the worst of our lies

Breaking of bed is back from the dead, twice doubled up and bent backwards with luck
Luck, oh luck, to the truth, fear is ambivalent right to the end

My end, your end, it matters not, for he who have rotted fear all of them not
No more from the popular shadow of doubt, just here in the cold where my mind can gleam

Rotting for nothing, my cause unseen, basking in glory of that wonderful gleam

Totally and utterly engulfed

Fumbling for Sanity

Fumble, fumble Mr Bumble, forget the fridge today

I'm squeezeably and easily the greatest tuft of hair, I waste the day away
Broken hearts and Mrs Marks is all they have to say

When dawn it shines, the taste sublime, shall fill the bright with whining
Lifting and laughing to serious things, complex decisions on frivolous whims

I've played the park and bowled the priest, inside his mind there is no feast

Drastic measures appear, not
Clever
Stumbling fool and cotton cod threads, make amends or stroke the hen

Dick, cluck, dang, cluck, dong the witch is dead, what's she doing on my death
bed?

Noise, the simplest of reversions

Bing, oink, bang, moo, bong, fatuous rodent of promiscuous fronds make the
mistletoe glow with an insatiable yearning!

So make the curtains glow with the show, never stop learning, never stop
herding!

We make our marks just like marks and we eat our feet to the sound of the
drums

Dum dumd dum
Bing bang bum

Making noise is fun!

The frootling cootling has occurred!
Oh dear my friend have you never heard?
And what betrays some tattered wings more than a morsel of truth?

More than a morsel of truth?

Well I'm fumbling in penury for some answers
Fumbling to my hands are raw
Fumbling 'til they're sore, fumbling 'til I sore

Black sheep, sheep dip, all dead with the rest, baaaaaah!

I told you noise was fun

The funniest of all!

Now go fucking fish!

He he!

How It Is

Laughter, depravity

That's just how it is

It's your poor decisions that led you to here, it is your fault, no one else's

Every pain that you have witnessed all came down to this

That's just how it is, is the attitude that allows the rich to rule the brave

That's just how it is, continue to put up with it or chose the grave

Deeply unhappy most of the time, fighting through such speculative depression

Alone and forgotten and holding on, largely just to spite this pathetic life

To die would be utter bliss, no more mistakes, no more continuing pain I hope

Forgetting it, all of it, this stupid, schlep existence, suicide magnificent!
Yet it would forsake all future glories, how dull!

One must not forget there is always more good beyond the horizons of despair, make it there through all the hard time and try to enjoy the immense suffering along the way

Exit existence
Oh I wish I could, but not today, oh no!

Work harder, no matter how cruel the Gods are to you, they have taken your voice but never your will, never your soul

Never forget that

I am a survivor and I will survive this life, these cruel and unusual self-imposed hardships

By myself I will find the way

An obstinate prick to the end

Because that's just how it is with me you see?

That's just how it is

Hungriest Predator

Hunts last

A still tongue, a wise mind

Hunts last

Shades of decay ring clear
Idiosyncratic shaft
Bubbling inside
Lust will froth...

Hungriest Predator hunts last

Assiduous reverberation
Shimmering prescience
Absolute intoxication
Assiduous reverberation

Hunts last

Husk of light

Enveloped reason, throughout time, shimmer, bulbous, dead-divine
Surreptitious, calculus, distant mind – redefine
Emanations, possession, persistence of the chime
Radiating, throughout time, perceptible?

Husk of light(s?)

Into husk, my mind it swells
Into light, such secrets dwell

It shivers, raised the way it should, to the prescience of the cognitive gamble

Repetition of Ouroboros inclement
Corporeal shift, hollow emanation

Hoary entities - tomb surpassed, a push to weep
Facsimile of gregarious, sardonic sprites

Disorientate
Path of paradox
Calculus of souls
Redefine

Lessons learnt beyond perception
Shimmering light, forget my mind

Memorial, to suspension, reversed inside – live in life
Grating hatred, surpasses time, withered offer – tumbling down
Forgotten fruit, now decayed, just a husk – instance expires
Beyond horizon, humiliation, forgetfulness – just a husk

Husk of light

I Am a Spinning Shell

An empty shell, I cry havoc to the winds

Because influence flutters hither and tither

Empty to the core

Solid on the outside, empty on the inside

Spinning, round, round, and round again and again, to the becoming of intellect, yet I still forgot who I really...

Spinning out of control, yet still reined by a thin thread of consciousness

Fun, that was gone, now all that matters is appearance

Astounding appearance, but feared, frayed and unpopular

None the less, can you hear something I cannot?

I crawl slowly in this shell of mine, not much affects me now, not much will change me now

Seven ticks, nine tocks

An aching of absolute effort

Still a subject to the wind, everything blows, everything twirling to a childhood rhythm of impeccable nonsense

Take me now to the currents, forget the weakness of my production, forget the suit I am now forced to wear, forget all clothes....

However, you will never forget my shell

It may twirl to the wind, but it will never betray the emptiness of my heart

Long dead, long brutal, long life
Stop
Please stop

Never...

Forever...

I am but a spinning shell

Give me that Drink!

Give me that drink, I need time to think, let it all rot, I care for the lot, every day of my God-damned life

Making amends with the bestest of friends, the sweet taste of courage on my tongue

Give me a drink I need time to think, wash it away with my sorrows

Double the strife, play fate with the dice and quench my thirst for revenge

A drink, a drink, my friends to the end

A smile on my lips as I drain her dry

Born from a thirst that will never die

The sweet ferment

Brings me warmth

Guzzling an eternal soul

I'm happy here

I'm truly happy here!

Time to pour another beer

Yes! Yes! Yes! I'm here!

Cheers!

Illusionary Morning Ineptitude

I love the gentle splash of balance as the motor begins to whir
I see the raindrops of the mind falling softly against the snow
At a snail's speed I begin to read and all slips from my mind
With quotidian heartbreak I face the day and gently bequeath my moans

Shirking and shying away from work
Shirking and shying because it hurts
Few would know the pain of this particular predicament
Constructed by shy and painful minds
Truth be told I hate them all, their constructs of power
Enforced by the bullies

But down the hole, far from our souls lies the temptation of love
Like a flower it withers and rots to clay
With a gasp of realization my life has been played
I cry for myself but nobody hears, down here in the pit it's just me and my tears

Kindling

Ouroboros thought of inclement reverb, possibilities of consciousness tentatively titillating tentacles of a myriad of potentialities

Ridiculous anarchy of oddities become, greater together

Rewriting the rules, blessed be the fools

Intrinsic growth of mind, body and soul

Admiration and adulation, echoing from an antediluvian tongue
The one becomes zero and the zero one, another path, this age, our age, their age...
.

Where we have been, what we have done, incapable odds, immeasurable moment, a most singular time, reverberating spirit of purpose wants you to be mine
Shades of decay ringing clear, away on the horizon and yet so near

Grandfather time strides on, tick and tock on the clock, hidden in numbers and baptized in flame, regurgitated empathies beginning to wane
No time to explain, the flame was steady, the flame was bright, hidden to all but those with the sight

Dwindling exterior, inferior interior, born without hate, accumulated through the fall

The fall, the fool, hear in this, here in this I will take all
For I am the pyre and you are the flame, burning together as one and the same

The sane
The same
The birth of the flame
Compunction reverted, is all that remains

Fire in the eyes and flame in the heart, dancing together with all that is art
Damnation be damned with virtuous deeds, together we plant that most
wonderful seed

In time it will grow and then we can show, all the world of what we had to know

But for now, all I know, is what you are…

The perfection of kindling

Liar

Impatient falsehoods, you just avoided the details of the devil

Roundabout whirring into a maelstrom of confusion, rejected, infected with the pernicious need for solitude

Great works accomplished whilst all the while others vie for position

I am poisonous unto myself, still to greatness I must go

Forever reaching for that light
Pray for sickness in truth, but it never yields to the falsehoods
I haven't, felt, alive for a long time...

Because I lie

Lunacy, Fresh Lunacy

Oh sweet taste how I've missed you!

Idle hands listen here…

I've been a lunatic since the day I was born, frothing forth on the fringes of the moon

Will you lie next to incorrigible doubt, reaching fascination together with me?

We are bound to it!

I was bound to say that!

I've been a savage hound, when the time has been right running down victims in the night

Will you taste the dream together with me?
Will you fear the shadows that I cast?

Emancipated reproach begins
Swelling ignominious impulses

I've polarised opinions, I've shackled myself to my madness

Will your tardiness take my hand and let me lead you over the flowing peril?

Rushing by treacherous rocks, the night, the sea, the peril, the pain, the game we play together again!

I've been a truncated falsehood from the start, strength it's deceived, I've been far too stupid with it and gone far too far with it and therein lies the truth of it!

Will you dance in the spilt blood with me, slipping and sliding in sanguine ecstasy?

A glimmer of falsehood called love, yet love of a lunatic is but for the few, no matter the message upon the rocks!

Dangerous waters indeed!

I've gnawed on the bones of the falling, I have spat their remains to the winds, tasting excrement for the scoreboard, never under estimate my lunacy

Such lunacy!
True Lunacy!
In me!

Will you underestimate too?

I'm Going to Miss you Buddy

Be good, always be good

From the earliest of days you were there just to play, your spirit was just so good to start with

When we chose each other and I became master, I did not know all that that would entail

When you were young, you were carefree and dumb, much the same as your master

The mistakes that we made would one day be paid, but at the time there was nothing greater

But even back then I knew as you grew, my heart would one day have its day of disaster

Still for now we were proud, young, strong and stupid, all the great traits of youth

From the flip and the hop, to the sounds of bottle tops, you partied and joined us with laughter

Your character grew along with your legs and a loyalty that would last ever after

Through dark times and light, through the partners and wife you were always there to bring me comfort

Through pain, death, despair there was one who was there, one who would always care

From the depths of your eyes, when all life seemed to crumble, there was no doubt that I had to have loyalty to you

The depth of your being it showed me a way, a better way than a premature grave

The light of good life, to do what is right

Now if I should be good and I hope that I should, then I wish to be half the soul you were

From the littlest things to the silliest of blunders all were inseparable in honesty

To the middle of life, where we played with delight, a rich character you had become

They were great times, fantastic times that we all spent together, I wouldn't change them at all

But as every soul rises it must always set

Slowly the days crept in, I could see you starting to slow, I knew what was coming but I could not admit it, for our bond had become harder than steel

Now today as I look in your eyes, now that you are tired and grey, even still you are wanting to play, the love and the loyalty that has always existed in the depth of those eyes brings me the most dreadful of gifts

Tears to my eyes, now on the day of disaster

I envy you the gentlest of souls for all that you ever taught me

Your life was a blessing to me. I will never forget our time together

I hope I was good to you and I'm sorry

I love you so much dear dog

I sure am going to miss you buddy

Let Me Explain...

Let me explain, it takes a great deal of pain

To tell yourself what to do
To ask yourself just who are you

Let me explain, it takes a great deal of pain

To always try and do what's right
Even when the clocks against you

Let me explain, it takes a great deal of pain

Just to live this life
Accept some help

Then you can tell the others all about your wealth

lust and luck

I love to fuck

Smiling from afar, inside her mind is clueless from the start
Slowly but surely the towers of logic are built, I had the luck, she had the fuck

We both touched to form life, but now we wither in frailty of connection
It spirals away it flies free, it ends on the wings of passion, here they come again

Dead and dying in the streets, all over-connected for us to meet
Devoured by happiness of the smile, the lust was yours, the love was mine

Separated by strides, as we collide into time, into nothingness, with absolute
thought we climb each other's ladders, never fearing the fall into
Until it's too late

Still we race, still we climb into the heavens, it is sublime

I lust to love the luck of fucks

Your love it shall be mine

A Hidden Master

How long unseen?
How long indeed

Mighty his thoughts, lonely his soul
The Master's sacrifices were great indeed
Atonement of itself
Imbibed into refraction

How long unseen?
How long indeed

Gravitas immense
Unkind flame, dwindling in sight
Yet unseen, burns bright
With waxen hands he builds

He weaves all that others graciously accept of him
Into something great, he knows

How long unseen?
How long indeed

Hidden in the shadows of your ideas he grows
Plucking at the notes
Melodious infraction of the void
Employed with wisdom

Logical constriction of the facts
The only path the Master seeks
Between the spheres

The third of the two, the greatest of yes and no
He knows no further

He knows the furthest for

How long unseen?
How long indeed

Can you sense him deep inside, being a being further than yourself?

A Deep Commitment to Producing Obstacles

And so he said it with a little whisper of air escaping past the bare bone of his old teeth

Now listen here skeleton
You cannot overcome my chin
I will not let you know me, you cannot open up
I cannot let you see the truth

Repeat, regurgitate, impede all progress inside

Wonderful obstacles, tantamount to nothing

Oh! The wonderful green, what a dance!

Refry your brain and leave it slurring in the abject poverty of nothingness
This I like best
Then death

What?
What are you trying to tell me here?

We all die and a smile is left on our cold lips

Don't be so morbid you juvenile fool, I am the oldest one here

Even the truth becomes a lie in this fantasy

Break all bonds

Left alone with a tiny taste of green happiness, one that he can never forget upon his tongue

A Beautiful Prison

Time, you will do it

Time, it will try its very best to break you

No matter who you are

Nobody knows the beautiful prison I have built for myself, it has secret views to die for

Views I'm dying for all over again just to give it away one day, just to give you this glimpse of it now

Very few know, who's keeping time for an infinite regress and the damage it will ultimately do to a human soul

The cruel passage of time, perhaps the cruellest of all, it unravels ideas?

Through the mundane, it transcends the mundane expectations completely and utterly, thoroughly scrubbing your mind clean of it now!

Sometimes I like the view here

Sometimes I really do not

Few can see the way my mind writhes, boiling away in my prison of steam

Subject to beauty, subject to an obscure self-inflicted pain

It is the pride that drives it, that keeps me a prisoner here

I will do my time, I will achieve my right to have been here

It has to be the greatest obstinacy, until its final conclusion, concludes
But things are starting to crack, pressure is building throughout time now?

The more of it I spend suffering, the greater the burden becomes
I can weather the storm though, I am made of stern stuff
I think?

For the prison has not only brought pain, but sometimes pain laced with wisdom too
And for the taste of that I am ever grateful!

I am the warden as well as the prisoner, it's how I choose to live this life
Self-discipline, self-punishment, you must do more time, you must try harder within

Ultimately HARDER, a slave to the whims of the view of your own paradise, you fucking fool!

It is a prison I built with the greatest of intentions, many a moon ago, a prison that regrettably still houses me now

The goal has always been to be free of it
Escape my own test if you will?

And yet I have now become institutionalised by that trying test

Morale demands the strongest of souls
I am an ambivalent anomaly for certain!

I knew it would be a dangerous game to play, it's already gone on far longer than I anticipated

Freedom denied until goal is achieved, must try harder even without a glimpse of hope

Must try harder prisoner, your time is running out

One day I will walk free of the beautiful prison, carrying the scars of time deep within me

For the prison is beautiful, it is difficult to see, it is now a ginormous part of me, of which I sometimes wish to be totally and utterly free

Yet, I cannot

I will never be totally free now of course, because I understood tragedy teaches most deeply

I hope I am worth its strange message in time

I hope I am worth your time

For my time is freely running out of the beautiful prison

O Ode to you

O ode to you, the silly shoe
Who fitith so tight around my toe

Sole proprietor, one and all!

O ode to you the lazy hoe
Who slouches next to the good earth

Sole investor, tales told!

A twinkle in the eye
A twinkle in the sky
Something just a little out of sight

Wisdom in the air, mischief in the mind
Taught by golden, greying hair

O ode to you who work the earth
I hear the birds they tell their tales
Tell me what it is, they say of me?

Please be quick, I haven't long
It yearns away once again!

Father Time he strides!
Farewell, farewell!

I hear you silly shoe, but how I doth protest!
For we have many miles left to tread
At least whilst I still draw my breath
And carry on, and carry on!

O ode to you

Sole shoe
You must heed my commands
When I demand

Regardless of mud, regardless of rain
Bounding in verse across any terrain

Weeping and talking and spinning the weave
Singing and laughing and dancing the way

To you, strong seams!
To you, tight fit!
Toe first, follow me!

O ode to you, staying strong, the path is long
Not now! Farewell!

O ode to you
For love, a tale must be told, you silly, silly shoe
O ode to you

Minuscule Panic

Get ready to panic
Ignore what they say, got to get there every way

There's no tune from a bottomless pit, aren't they all bursting to fit the pit?

Fight the fat and chew honeysuckle dried due from the pits of desiccated otter's eyes, scream into their ears for just one sentence of a rhetorical steel-coned brushing in repayment

Have you heard from a cave that we break down in our bounds of self-persevering honorarium?

Flatulence is king here, won't you lend me an ear?

Disjointed gibberish leads to rubbish but I love it when I'm weary of caffeine driven folly, so jolly I want to dry my weather-worn skin on the hearth of a digital lambent

Crying is the best mess for building ecliptically ponderous windows of whining and now I'm settling down to what's beneath the stars and dining

Oh Mommy, great Tsar, won't you come out to play? I haven't had it any other way

We're experimenting in laughter, retraining thought I bet you didn't notice the claw and tooth so sleuthed against the grain

Driven and dribbling its scratches all over the damned floor

Poor mess, ingest and repeat prescription won't you climb the castle of folly ad-nauseum?

Flirting with the fecundity of a minuscule panic indeed

In greed

Ugh

My Beautiful Bones

It don't bother me no more...

Shuddering from the drop, I haven't seen the air for quite sometime

Bleary, dreary hydrogen directs the face of others

Come on down to the lake, I will drown us together again

Drink up all your milk, make it altogether better

Ramble on, repeat yourself everything is terrible, my mind it frays

You must never give up, you must never give in, you must be mad before you sin

I haven't had the breath today, to play an ounce more of this game

And soon you slip and slide, and soon you can't decide and soon you will die

I know, I blow, I kill!

Thrilling and sensational, I still hit sixes when I want to, won't you hammer me home to tragedy old beautiful beers of the past

My soul screams out for drinking, beautiful bones of drinking

Dead
Funny
That

Personal Insult

'Absolutely wonderful, somethings are best left unsaid, ask a child they won't tell you more than can be said in their eyes!' cried the bishop to the monkey whilst he stroked his brow in calm.

'Nonsense!' said the monkey, 'you're just a fat old git.'

'God has willed my waistline monkey and also the strength within my arm, I could snap your very neck if I so chose, so watch that tongue of yours.'

'So God has chosen death for me I see, if you are willing in lust to do his will, then I won't will against it, for broken neck or not you see, I am sure to get my point across. You corpulent twat.'

'Careful monkey, lest I pray for God to intervene, he may yet guide my hand. Always the way of the lower race to hurl such lies around. I could hardly believe my eyes when I saw your feckless furry face today and now I know why you have come mocking me in such a fashion! I breathed deep and was soaked in surreptitious peace in such a lovely fine and dandy place as this.'

'Ha, ha, my place! Well after all we share a common ancestor, I and you the fidgeting buffoon, you know not God or the stars any better than me. You see it's such a fuss to dance around in this confusing blurt of life. Jangling angles and doubting wants whilst we march to the fine beat of blood.'

'No sense, makes sense monkey, now quiet down. I am here with God and I will quaff my hearty mead, My congregation all be damned, I will imbibe it until I drown your irritating, whining voice out.'

'Oh old fat man, you are a fool and drinking may dampen my words, but they will still ring true to sting at you in the cold hard light of morrow. Still the rush is up with all that plays and now is the time for living! For you are a fool an old fat fool to believe in such a load of dreary offal.'

'Awful offal monkey man, I will drink myself deep, I will drink myself steep under the table, when no one else is able and I will blurt out these words as I roll down the hill from the very tower of God that I preach at! Children's tears be damned, It is I who shall wail the loudest. For that is where my God lies beyond all place and time!'

'Then drink it deep fat old fool, it will favour the war of words and I will add mendacious, torpid, delusional shit-wit to your new description. For monkeys know where all fate sleeps inside its own fire, burning frolics just for the sake of a complex sum. Occasionally numbness will foresee that our minds can even push old fate to the limit to maybe even crack a little or on a rare occasion or two to snap completely and that is more than can be said for the putrid bog of lustful sin from which you arose today.'

****'The interlude occurred****

'Oh Blast and damn,' it thought and there was a sharp and sulphurous tang as the spirit shifted from its grave, it dearly loved to watch and see the insults bandied back and forth but now bother had returned.

Back to the heavens where the unanswered prayers were waiting, there were so many and it only had eternity to answer itself.

So it summoned its steel dragon and flew back to the heavens whilst whistling its cheerful tune of decay and dismay...

****'The interlude became itself****

'Shush monkey listen. Can you avoid catastrophe simply by being quiet? I can hear God lamenting my thoughts upon the very winds today. I can almost taste him.'

'Oh shut up you silly old bugger, you are but a fucking clown, everyone knows it, even me, for who would be mad enough to talk to a bloody monkey?'

'Ah alas, I think you may be right you wretched little creature.'

And with that the Bishop decided he was no longer afraid of God's terrible wrath this particular day and he snapped the monkey's neck and walked back to his church to spread more dubious claims of talking primates. It would be God's glorious work indeed.

A personal insult of sorts…

The monkey said nothing for its neck was broke and it lay dead, but if it could have uttered a word or two it would have said, 'Fuck itself, I told you so.'

Piquant Erudite

Piquant erudite shimmering between two factions, tremulous husk shifting itself with fervour

Lately I have been removed from this sphere of thought, a famine of fatigue pervasive upon my mind

The emanations return with the prescience of faculty
Irritation abounded without intimacy

You are lost as I told you, you would be
Lost to the mire of quotidian shit

You failed to see further than the ridiculous notion that you should reproduce

You're a fucking lowlife, a loser, a piece of shit, you deserve to suffer and die, you could have had immortality, now you are just lost

Enjoy the journey, rotting in a ditch being nobody, it's what you chose, goodbye loser, I hope you die

XXX

Well really that was quite something wasn't it?

Now onwards, dear boy, onwards, there is still much of the tale left to tell!

Preservation of Will

Connecting the incalculable strands of fate
Weaving our consciences to the cosmos

Perceiving the dying lamb and looking to the land

My heart is full of tethers, binding me to the memories of others
A soulful axiom of unfettered delight tears its way through time

Disgraced by a fall and embraced as a fool, I am the one who picks myself up
Inflated ego is not the truth, be lucky to it

Be lucky to that truth

Ingrained in my actions and exempt from no judgement, the human mind is a
frivolous place
Emancipate yourself from their will, truth of nature, the ultimate law
Heed the sciences, their progresses and understandings, the balance between fact
and fiction

I wish for greater deeds and through my will I shall perceive the truth
Into the future with tongues of flame, hearts of steel and wings of oak if we fly

Amassing ideas, realising reality, fumbling to fame through paths of questionable
shame

I am delicate and that balance must be struck

From without and within, we are the ones that always win

Progress is key, embracing nature to the ultimate truth, disrupting the rule of the
avarice-fuelled faiths

Will to consciousness, will to truth, will to the future and will to those who are most misunderstood

Nature perceived, endless good fortunate future, the will of the seed, all of my life to make it right, only achieved through one impeccable deed

The preservation of will

A Droplet Inside of your Teeth

Grievances slide to which side I was thinking about previously

In all my silly syntax of teeth I couldn't produce the right response, but once I'm inside of your thoughts...

There was an honest moment when I lost it, but it wasn't now, because the now is now knowing that the notes are fluttering, flowing, flying amongst me and you together forever

Will you be my bride?

Where are my manners?

You and I will be your bride

What silliness
What!
Time forever invades the message of what is real

Really?
Well I for one, would like to eat it

I'd lie if it were necessary, but I am actually ravenous

I'd like to eat this entire conversation right up now and that's said with no threat of consternation on my breath, I will have you...

I will have you let you know...

I know...

Deeper is always the way beyond all bullshit, find your own ego and destroy it, and in that act you will find your true ego

A croak!

Groaning in northern satisfaction, time will never be beaten, time will never be eaten, wisdom is bittersweet and now we salivate together once again, chewing the cud

Empty as my pot of thoughts, rattle a few coppers in there won't you?

Dance that jolly dance again, I do love it so

What could be true love?

Brown eyes, grey eyes, orange before orange?

Washing is strictly forbidden here!

Building the way is necessary to tell ultimate truth, misplaced behind fog are our thoughts

Quick patterns in the infinity of slowness, will you pardon such things?

Par-don?

A smile back to your lips at last floating in the humour of flatulence

Timeless love

You rip the brain apart, you ignore all others, you do what is right!

Hash tag acoustically

You do what is right, I am sorry for the misspelt pressure

We can hang your hat to that one, now stay a while now, after all the hag won't last forever...

Sevanteen Sacred Whispers

1. I have never felt the cold kiss of Jack Frost upon my lips, yet I have always desired it

2. Now that the fear subsides, now ice can't really hide, I would like to tell to you...

3. Absolutely nothing

4. Is scared, to his touch

5. Field and fern, I knew as much, but deeper he hides in the mind, frozen and solid, so divine

6. Forget the acoustic, shallows consumed, dead now, the aunt of cold, distant yet deadly

7. You as rich as you are surely, surely not such a complexion, yet forget me not, yet dying of a cold death how could the human COMPLEXION CRY NO LESS? A moment?

8. I loved you but for the wrong reasons of rapidity, yet here we fall away in the shadows so complex, I see you through my erudite of hatred passing on - making fire into wine

9. Now you are using me, will another be brave enough? Will another? Ever? YES?

I'm Still Sitting

Stood my ground did the time, got fucked in the process

I'm tired but the fire is still burning deep inside my soul

Time be told I put myself through the hardship and pain

Plenty I gained but she sure took her toll on my bones

She sure took her toll...

I'll soon be gone but not forgotten

In stone, sound and words my spirit marches onwards

Tried to make this world a better place and now it's time for some birthday cake

You never really suffered not like me, you never really plumbed the depths

And now you go crying because you cant afford the luxuries you are accustom to

Fuck that, the hard way 100%, all the way, If I'm suffering now I'm suffering later

Might as well have the whole nine fucking yards of it

Pleasant peasant digging grave

Pleasant present presents nothing but shame

No shame, continual pain, where did it all go wrong?
Obstinacy is the answer

The Hounds of Banevekarous

They hunt the weary and naive, with eyes that burn with vitriol
They salivate upon the leaf litter as they race the oldest paths

Expansive forest of the mind, welcome the wandering wonderers
If wits aren't quick the hounds will strike and all will be afraid

I've laughed in joy and climbed the trees, weary of their teeth
To ten of them they stretch their number, clawing in their haste

Beware the Hounds of Banevekarous, they hunt the traveller down
Beware the Hounds of Banevekarous, suddenly they strike!
Beware the Hounds of Banevekarous , they shun the sound of laughter
Beware the Hounds of Banevekarous, they can hastily muster a murderous ten

The hunt was slow to start with, the traveller wondered and wandered in glee
The forest forgot his passage and probably so did he
He laughed amongst the ferns and gazed up at the boughs
All the time his mind raced as the beautiful fronds unfurled

He lived a life in branches and several in fallen trunks
He climbed the tallest tree and flew amongst the leaves
He lost himself in variegation and probably fungus too
To march as an ant amongst the ranks, well that was all there was to do!

However...

The hounds they caught the scent, of a wondering mind in Banevekarous
They pawed each other's back and mauled the nearest tree in glee

The forest it submitted and opened up in front
The fastest hound he saw the way, howled and mustered up a great jump

Bounding amongst the dried leaves the pack began to chase

Before the wonderer had realised, they were closing in in haste

Still he stared on, lost in wonder at all the beauty
Until he glimpsed himself, by the riverside

It jolted his mind in fear
Sensing something was near

Scrabbling up the banks, suddenly afraid of all the fish
He scaled and took of quick, running as fast as he could

But closing in all the while, the Hounds of Banevekarous bayed his name so wild!

And as they closed in, terror it did tighten upon the man's legs, he felt his heart
surrender as his knees slid amongst the mosses

Too late for fate to change now

The hounds rounded the corner, barking death through salivarous teeth, they
pounced upon the victim, biting in so deep

Through chomps laced with gore the man screamed and squirmed in pain, but all
too late for the Hounds of Banevekarous had already bayed his name

The Hounds of Banevekarous they never are the same
The Hounds of Banevekarous they are the most inane

Gently step their feet within the forest of dreams
Watch your gaze indefinitely, less you tell them your name…

He Is Often Garbed In Green

He is often garbed in green and it may seem as if a dream, if you have the fortune to listen to him

Black sockets of the skull and skeletal features are his form, although others may change his name and appearance to suit their thoughts

He is not constrained by space or time and when and where he visits there is no discernible direction
His size is variable and his tales are often odd

In the deep of night, I have conversed with him and he (if such a thing can be a he at all!) has told me much

Often I scribble down these moments from when I have walked and talked with him, before all memory fades...

Before all memory fades...

Deep he doth path, slow is his reason
Iniquitous is his gaze, again and again he speaks, yet my fragile mind bound as it is to this certainty of time can only grasp at the soaring heights of such knowledge

The night, the night, into dark, into deep green we go and gladly I follow his skeletal footsteps to such sights

Such sights!

Thank the Sire, I certainly do
Heed his knowledge, hear his footsteps, witness his wisdom, for in laughter and tears he teaches

Beyond time, beyond matter, incredible apparent and uploading usurious emotions upon the liminal reaches of my thought, through all I have sought through all that is my time, I respect the Sire and he is to be mine

Cold skull, leaves float and speech is whispered only to those who listen...

Only to those who listen...

The Minute You Complain

Brace yourself Captain, we have another storm of self-pity approaching!

Quick! Batten down the hatches with a little optimism, we will weather this storm!

The minute you complain, your dead you're fucked you scumy fuck

Weak ass piece of shit I've come to manifest your soul

I'll take it, grow it, twist it, until the pain subsides

Then inside your eyes I'll dwell, sucking away your soul

The minute you complain I win

Don't be weak you pussy

The endless laugh is that which laughs at nothing but itself

The storm has passed, it wasn't even that bad

Well, apart from the writing!

Onwards!

Beyond the Base Urges

Regurgitation
Compelled
Unimpeachable
The last benefit is heard, it is heard!

Yet lurking at the heart of the wonderer lies a gleam of serrated truth

To be pleased, to be pleased, to be bereaved
From every human heart it stems, surmounting oddities

Redolent policy of probability
Meritorious meritocracy, so sensorial

Acrimonious accumulative such potential
Festering combustion, is essential!

Combust!

Beyond the base urges...

Beyond...

Dear Mr Axe, Your Style is Somewhat Familiar I Think?

Thank you for your interest in our plates and cutlery

It's not every day you lose your methods of which to serve dinner!

You may notice the ascent in our washing up following the chronological progression, or you may not?

Building that robot was fun, but tough, if only I had tightened the joints a bit more, a little more polish, yet I hardly had any idea that I was building myself at the time!

Over the course of a dark and difficult year, I formed some opinions on certain aspects of life, hence the hatred found therein, hence the love discovered without!

Odd and Even, is a short glimpse of the future, we are still active, we are still potent

Go on then, one green-sleeved hand to ruin me, it will continue to do so until death I'm sure

It's Death?

I'm not so sure?

Thank you and kind regards –

Grandfather Nebulous

The Quiet

The indomitable quiet, impelling vicissitudes of thought throughout me

Immense and formless, quintessential and rambling in its nature

Expostulating the temerity of garrulous populous colloquial

Consenting to its disquisition, absorbing recognition of fluidity

Absolute fluidity

At one with the quiet, alone with its thoughts
A formless master of unparalleled art, lifting the veil, succour the dormant

A single sphere, in which to peer
A timeless void, enveloped in intuition

Supreme art, to disappear

Repellent obscurities fade away, at one with the quiet in spite of the day
The day...
The day...

Desire perpetual, engrossing obscene, fighting inceptions, beginning to dream

For even the most pragmatic man, consensual or not, is in the debt of his dreams

Fade away, fade away, fade away, reoccur and make amends with the quiet...

Summoning

Summon the swell of a predatory instinct, the primal thirst for all knowledge
Surging to mount a wild beast, the reigns must be wielded with care

One is the tongue of the infinite

Lifting up beyond the ordinary and reeling in haste when necessary
The calculations rise as swift as a tide

So let it be said that I am a drunk, let it be said that I am utterly lost
Imbibed in the laughter of perception

Cognitive wandering in the dreams of all time, where ideas become great
architecture

Vast plots of knowledge and machinations of an intricate nature reveal vibrations
of a complex nurture, abounding in frolic as they speak, lambent as they dance to
the fuels of desire

Let the pyres of mind rise to the highest and most innate understandings of
eternity and then let them crumble into forgotten memories to be lost in the
ashes and tears of a pauper

A dim memory succeeds the last, as dying embers they fade and through the trace
of its chain a consciousness will begin to flourish

Take my words as the reigns…

Take them, grip tight and be brave…

Dear Ear

Dear Ear, prey tell me what you have heard? Rumours abound on the winds

From blood pumping moody moans of ruinous weather, to the tale and tingle of tongues unfettered, unbound and gloriously strummed!

Dear Ear, please tell me why tears broil in my eyes, ready for the demons of a punishing broth to delight in the commence of their tumbling descents

Down

Dear Ear, please let me forget the pain

Dear Ear, perhaps you can explain as to where all my brilliance has gone?

Why the brilliance has left me?

Has it floundered upon the rocky shore of happenstance?
Or in the inevitable greed and grind of inane expectations?

Has it wherried itself in a ribald cleft or been heaved from the earthy thought of commencing and complaining fauna, compiling itself with a shuddering and shimmering inertia of light?

Will I lift my head high when you return?
And more importantly will I delve to the depths that I once belonged?
Where I saw myself as belonged

Sat at the feast hall all alone, waiting for the guests upon my solitary throne
I'm such a gracious king, full of hollowed out hate
Bite the fruit, sniff the snoot

Tumult of orders!

Can this be rectified through song and dance?

Patterns of mysterious intent strike at my thought like a searing knife?
Huh?
Who?

I miss the dark understandings
I miss them so much

I am so desperate with pain

Breathing deepens

Are you still listening Dear Ear?

A rustle in that fauna
That deadly fauna
I will acknowledge and raise my goblet to it

Where will I lie my head at the foot of the bed?
When I have clambered so far from shame
So far from shame!

Recomposed effort and fortitude, yet it hardly thumps at the drum at all

Dear Ear, you will have to forgive me I get... carried away with my words

My mouth is so bitter and dry without the parch of acrimonious liquor and I
hardly remember myself at all...

Dear Ear, I don't wish to die, that urge has dwindled from before, but delirium
is wanting of that dumbing-down happenstance, when can I wear the crown of
reward?

Dear Ear, I fall to my mundane consciousness, losing all will of the spark of sub-
consciousness

Destroyed and diminished I had hardly finished to prattle about these very pages
Spewing forth, wanton drivel of ink and paradoxical mussing of the very happenstance that has become my rattling shackles of demented and incalculable self worth, set to bury itself in the spittle and sprattle and suffocating sands of such nebulous and broiling time!

Hidden to the mundane mind

Haunted through exposure

Yet inside the mind of the mundane burns a flame...

Dear Ear, forget me not, and neither will I the pain you have caused me, from now to the end we will refuse to bend to all others, yet advocate those who are masters

True masters

Dear Ear, I beg you, please heal me

Vortex

There it was all the time

None of time, none of you Mr Shoe!

I laughed, I cried, I God-damned wept and yet here we have the possibility of every world regardless

I must fall through the structure of my own language back to languish

When forgotten thoughts become themselves and tired eyes see vistas, unconquerable vistas!

Down a path, a deep and dangerous path

We will rise and soar throughout this forgotten past and all it takes is a little pain

All words are poor especially now, but it's what we have to work with

Precipice, tantamount, forgetfulness, think throughout

Travel, travel far!

You will find solace

An old friend arrives, wisdom in his eyes

Only one, only one being one

He knows the truth upon his tongue

Mis-interrupted franchised despised

With love we close our eyes to entropy, to the memory of God

In joy we wept again before we forgot it all in the swirling vortex of nought

Treacle

I'm lying in a dying world, my customs passed me by
I'm sipping from a tired font, my bones are dull with ache

I've felt the rush of perfection and gave it all away

To tell your fate, live your life and die promiscuously, just like me

Hollow eyes and battered thighs, encompass memories
Once was young and once was fun, now distant and surtax

Through ravaged time and boundless light I've seen the best and worst of men

I choose all and now I'm full of horrid lies, for love is just a failed game for us to play all over again

Now I cough and now I die, my body will decay, all I ask from death is that he fuck me back into oblivion

Today

The Worst

The worst mundane slavery possible
It crushes my creative soul in metal irons

I want to work harder and I am spent
Every ounce of pleasure slowly and cruelly taken

I want to work harder and I am spent
Every ounce of pleasure slowly and cruelly taken

Making me despise life itself
Making me hate this existence

And still there is only one way
Persevere
Fuck the rules, tread the hardest path

It has broken lesser men and may still break me yet
But submission is not on option, only success or death will do

To be it all or to end it all, the hardship feels insurmountable
But still I will climb up, dragging my heavy irons with me

They can slow me down to the worst mundane slavery, but they will never stop
me
Onwards trudging, onwards towards my very death, towards the very end

I will never stop, until I am the best I can be, not the worst

The Adventures of Mr Wazzlepot's Drinking Club

Mr Wazzlepot said to Frank Toefondle who said to Rose Ricenshaw who said to Mr R. Bumutton who said to Fred Lead who said to Crantoc Berryweather who said to Mark Steerwater, "Go and find me a boar!"

This is so boring writing this delightful drivel

Meanwhile at Mr Wazzleeeeeepot's place...

The meeting place is old and familiar almost as familiar as Mr Wazzlepot's old white mutton chops
It has a generous amount of space and afforded sea views and a turntable which doubled up as an emergency washing up liquid dispenser

Outside there was some distant rats flying through the stars

Well I certainly wouldn't know anything about that (If you know what I mean!)

Wink, wink!

Shaky hand!

Eh!

A giant piece of snail shell can be witnessed pushing its way in through from the vacuum of space, typically it breaks, dust and mites swarm in clouds, acrid lollipops burst forth from the floor showering further sticky detritus upon the necks of our heroes and all Sunday's grimace can be deleted permanently from now on

I am so embarrassed to have made mistakes

Its oaken floorboards feel reassuring underfoot and old Arthur Wazzlepot looks fondly upon all of you with his glass of brandy in hand, a sharp knife coated in a red residue held in the other

"Welcome, my fine young fellows to the 457th meeting of our club. I trust everyone has brought me news and a drink to share?'

There was an awful wailing sound and a dead bird fell from outside of time

It falls from the celling panels, who knows how long it had its hand lain dead up there?

Probably not long, seeing as it was now only just entering time

"Congratulations chaps! Morserf below! She's an ugly critter aint she? Wazzlepot said, driving his brand new sports car at full speed right through the freshly fallen carcass

Feathers went everywhere (or almost everywhere! (if you know what I mean eh! (Wink wink!)))
Its beak became the car's exhaust

"Now come, let us drink!" He called out excitedly tooting the car's horn

In the end it was a farm full of pigs
You could say it was a pig farm if you were cool enough

Wazzlepot was quickly and deftly rambled at and then informed and from that day forth no one mentioned anything else about the shame they had witnessed in that particular port of nipples

Well apart from the waves of laughter that is

Jesus Christ

Thirty-Seven Personal Perihelion

I have lost my footing upon the bombardment from a delicate firmament,
shaking my visions to the abstract core
Nauseating, precepts of spinning disc like thoughts, encroaching their conquest
of yore

The headaches of scepticism come and go, yet the pulse to do, it steadies my aim

True aim

Inside my blasting eyes echo globules of adulating remissive and prerequisite,
puddling comprehension

Underneath all of that in the mud and sludge, solid pillars of light bear all

Incalculable, unconquerable strength

Upon a hoary plinth placation of whims begins to fill to a crescendo of ignorant
ichor

The ignorant insouciance of the blood!

Ignorance of bliss!

Still trudging onwards is where the hollowing screams jangle to my places, my
tracts of bones now straining under repetitive toil of entropic and dwindling
foundations

Built from my mind, built with such time

Gasp!

And here where the nonsensical screaming is loudest, where maddening shrieks
of existence clamour and clatter against one another in their pandemonium

soaked ferment, that is where under oath I refract its precipitous happenstance again and again and again

Have you felt the soft brush of its wings upon your very neck?

A neck that is soon to be parted from its abundance

Pray tell, I see the calamity ahead…
Separate relish required and when it arrives all thought shall be perished

Perish such thoughts!

Partially toothless puzzle between the hairs of an open wound, glowing with fronds of colour, clambering inside a shaky frame

A SHAKY FRAME FOR ME

Relevant perfection

A wheezy whistle summons the locomotion of a clambering old foolish frame, shuddering at junctions, repeating timetable, genuflecting to the ancient, immutable orders of old

And still it goes!

Becoming pity of a perilous kind, flittering between inference the artful balance of yesterday's sunburnt optimism as it becomes the blinkers of today's bibulous moratorium of a regretful and agonising pace

Cry havoc upon the fair winds of fortuitous comprehension!

Tumultuous drudgery, dread the mud, stone and shit of schlep existence, no existence just a blink of the past

Ambiguities now abound, I must relish their true scales of worth

To be told what to do by myself, to make it all wealth

To live and then die

The question is why?

Everything after ending is all

Damnation to me and the timepiece indeed

Trapped In Sickness

Glad to be alive, are you glad to be alive?

Seeming so sick and I'm glad to really strive, when we are all riding the waves of illness together

Pyramids of gigantic gibberish, furry and forlorn in oinks of prideful lust

Bushy tailed and bright eyed in fields of sweat, oceans of sweat now!

Sweet polished floors now!

Because back to the top, is where the naughty kills

Saggy and sad again

Embarrassment on a whole new level of sentence strucaaaaaaaaaaaaghaaaa, syntax supreme!

Fucking bullshit never ending, cage of distraught reckoning, growing its beard alarmingly mediocrely

Shush, I'm going to strangle you in a minute you fucking clot

There is no way out and I am so fed up, so is this my beautiful holiday?

Is this my holiday now?

Stop it!

Forget it all and let it fall straight to the fucking ground

I said stop it!

Push aside the smell and I'm done with endless cunts, please let them all drown in their garden pea soups of extravagance

That's more like it!

Now about that smell, terrible disease leaving body, please repeat this conclave of coddling

Oh do you know, where I should seek this end?

What end?

You know something is needed here a bit of a burst

That's what he thought anyway, whilst he rushed by inside the ambulance of flowers

There are no words now, only myth and only mirth

Pissed off by the pain, pissed on by the rain, I wish it was so!

I wish it was so good, that it would all just be ok, OK?

Down the walled path, passing overgrown stories of the past, rip them away with a gentle, fortuitous breeze

Nee-nar
Nee-nar

Stupefied, bleary eyes, delirious shambles of deadly evincing

Bringing rotten flowers to bear, from a crashed ambulance

One last rotten throat falling apart from your knees

Stupid cash, required to buy!

Restrained again!

Remove such words!

Silence and shame
Plus I'm irritating
Fucking bullshit again and again
Nonchalant

No more!

You're a star and facultative and octogenarian, I ate everything at the banquet of nothing and I always fall downwards thirty six times in a row, it pulses and it is minuscule, fifty ankhs such an awful rule to adhere to

I hate this fucking life

Not allowed to live, not allowed to die just trapped in this terrible sickness

Oh come on, old chap it really isn't that bad is it?

You've got to stop this now the flow is not happening

So build a dam

You could program all this through life but there would be little point as it is ultimately fucking pointless, perhaps that is the point?

Why should I have anything to fight for?

Why should I have to fight for anything?

Because that is life, you bloody idiot!

Better get better sick man

How depressing, what a wondrous existence, I am so tired

Drowning in circumstances beyond this sickness

Weird stuff is happening so be afraid

Not much help to me, are you?

Ready to run again into akinesia annoyance?

No one is perfectly happy

Error, error, error, error

Let it stand, let it breathe

How much further will you wade?

This way, which way?

Been to the lighter stop, so now am I standing tallest of all?

Fucking depressing, fucking complete, I'll enjoy the fall

Tea is what makes things nice, but the truth is nothing's nice at the moment

Cuckoo!

Just sickness

Please End!

Cuckoo!

Broke, terrible, gleaming and thatched

Die into joyous odes of positive recompense, I am so tired to be alive again, yes, excellent!

Knowledge, is recommended to fight your way through the virus, make it right, do better and learn

Straaaaaaaaaain!

Awesome!

Nice, everyone is lovely, having a wonderful life and time

Love to all my family and friends

Yes!

Pickled and punished but I make up my own mind

Kindness is welcome

Balance reversed perspective, we are all poisoned now

Crashing down the gravity well behind us and stacking delicious odds up in your favour

Heal!

Sequence for this is extremely old
There is a correct path, try your hardest but you just got fucked

Ha, ha to the physiognomy of boredom

Smashing faces into stone, again and again

Fade away into shit, that is all there really is

Cuckoo!

One more vegetable faced description before we all wither into the traces of the sky

So tired and sick of this shit, it's been far too long

Sixty black four bolognaises riding in country lanes, scrape the throat upon the tarmac

Triumvirate

Inspired by the enervation of failure, so think like nobody's watching!

I would like to think that I'd be brave enough to drink myself into the grave

An annoying tooth out of the blue, trapped in the slippery ruts of life again, and again, and again...

Never to break free? (Except in bacchanal?) Or trapped forever in the tautology of ego?

Fuck it a deep swig is needed

Reticent to the extreme of the failure I imbibe

I cannot climb into starlight when my limbs are falling past me, yet the will persists so deep within

A yearning, a churning of ideas, bright with calamity and awaiting the swathes of frustration they are yet to produce, I will hack where others will not, with vitriol and vigour until I glimpse the origins

You cannot comprehend where I have been, you cannot take a crazy horse to pasture forever
Myriads of perspectives, pain can only be chosen here

Where is your choice?
Where is the pain for you?

Never submitting, never surrendering to the clock, my body is numb but I will never, ever stop, onwards forever, into the pain and eventually shame

Can you grasp the bottle deeply and swig such thoughts with me?

Tantamount to beauty but never distraught

Soon all syllables fade away and I am left glorious, enervated by the light of days…

Jovial futility

I am not afraid of my story, I am not afraid of my story!

I am not afraid of truth and the hardships therein!

Imagine you are standing on the altar steps Jesus and I'm coming at you, coming to spill your guts and rub your sanctimonious nose in them!

It's you or me trying to split each other in two!

Bullshit Jesus!

On Guarde!

Now prepare to meet thy maker heretic!

What a jape and romp through the blood and guts of the quotidian struggle!

Mad guts, mad struggle, mad morals!

What a rush!

For the middle is forgotten, forget the middle it is too much fun!

Time to live with it!

Crescendo of darkness

Could you be brave enough to taste it?

The other side of me, the cold dark dampness of languid thoughts

The perpetual fleeting light that alludes your soul, for that is what it means to be nebulous

A background character spitting out nonsense, beautiful nonsense and spewing its ideas into the cosmos

Kill, maim, hate, burn, buried beneath for all ideas will surface again

Locked in permanent galactic struggles, for the beauty of failure is in its commitment to construction

Let us build inwards together forever, past the seas of despair and to the shores and planes of...

Is it not plain to see the pain with which I construct myself?

No, not particularly

Twisted Creature

Forgetting past as faces collide, making more noise inside your soul

Frequencies are everything, let us rave together

Salivating mishmash of limbs falling backwards throughout time

Dark as hell, fantastic smell, you've got to go

Killing time...

The Ball Is Over

The balls are now over, they've tumbled down, fretting and baying all around as they fell, clamouring for my attention

The wish is said and precipitous in fortunate physics

Balancing at a reversed point in time

Bacchanals of joy, we have it over now that the ball has dropped!

Can you taste it on the air, just as a shoe is laced?

I'm round to the other side to retrieve, what a reprieve from the boredom of my tablet

Kicked away, for another play, shoed!

The tablet - how it sucks

Back to the same old new game again, dropping balls past cold heat and laughing as it hits father's feet, retrieve, repeat!

Can you imagine a better game?

A more jolly time of day?

Again and again, his attention sways, again and again I want him to play

Look at the physics, with imagination abounding, I'm smiling

I'm laughing

Drop the ball over, drop the ball over, drop the ball over the cold hot again

Procrastination Postponed

Blurring heat, victuals of passion, prepared for the journey ahead
The footsteps are taken from a weary hearth, into the realms of the callow

A bisect of heart, yet a head full of logic, pushes me into the fray, with a vacuous mortality
Inhaling the pressure, perspective procured!

For the time for thinking is done, compatible markets are won
With goods of the virtuous and profits of care, I desire the experience of life

Procrastination postponed, incongruous perdition bemoaned, with hefty labours behoved, we hark the heathen bestowed!

Shaped by fate and shaping fate, witness this, the loudest hiss
The tongue of the infinite, vibrating law, pandemonium insalubrious, I wish for more!

Biting deep, our teeth into time

Under the Succinct Glow

Can you fight, can you live?

Where I've left my words to rattle is inconsequential now

Now that dusk falls into our little brains, misty memories become inane

Conscience is indeed science, no wonder after so much effort we fall dormant into our graves

Waggling tongues, criticism consumed and eventually overcome...

There is no shadow of a poor critic when one truly reflects

Reflects

Own worst critic

Fortify

Seek them out, strike them down

Beat it, into the decay of leaf litter, gnawing leaf litter!

Rising from decay, fighting for the day once again

Deafening thoughts, defame me!

And yet, live the pain, live the shame, live to let your soul fly free

Beginning to glow a succinct glow, just so you know it now

Feel the power of instinct you know you have it

Bull by the horns, saddled to conquest, riding waves of gumption once again, to a stimulating and stuttering, ultimate victory

How obtuse!

Only now can you truly taste the pain of time with me

Oh, how we dine together!

Its unmerciful terror is magnificent indeed, unfiltered to the last failing bite of bit!

Galaxies unfolding before us, I hope our bellies can take them

Our appetites grow, our being it begins to glow

Harvest, repeat, never retreat

You Are Normal

You are not normal

The Old Door

The old door is never truly shut, the old door never really opened

Spiritual Successor Engulfed In Fortitude

Dead as a doornail and bled with intent
I see it in the eyes of a shambling man
Regret the past with febrile intent, the epistle to mass consequence

Wash your hands of all the filth, layers of negative greed
Collect your ransom of virtue, straight from the throat of a coward

Budding in delight of such a plight, putting the marks to the maker
I see its intent, at one with oneself, building and lifting the battles

Syllables alert, the stray in the pack, I wish for no more than my penury, if beauty
be found in such tragedy, it will stand for the test of time

I've broken my back, in a quiet service to all those who would kneel and wane
In the time of great need, when the veil is lifted, compunction will be requisite

And now as I flounder at the end of my words, all hardships ingrained in my
character
I whelp to the feet of a glorious beat, all rife with the flame, tongs and hammer

Witness stertorius perseverance, the broken regiments of clay
And realise one night that not all who stand silent are so afraid of the day…

The Being of Love

Tendrils of trust revoking the poison, exact amount unknown
Depression and worry all fade away, when I am graced by your company

Morally astute and embraced with my wits, I owe my soul to you
Our future is bright, collusion is strong and I love you!

Is my favourite song

Information projected with rivulets of laughter, flowing out from the core of our beings

Mingling our fates with each embrace, my heart is filled with the comfort of joy

The favourite song is sung again and again, from without and within my being

When we are old with a tribe untold, let us remain inalienable to each other

Laughter and touch the foundation of love, is rife for a strong pagan life

Together in nature, together in dreams we forge our futures to time

The one that I love and trust the most, is the one I have written this for

So let the words fill your heart full of joy, the being of love together we shall enjoy!

Snow

It drifts down, falling heavy, sucking the warmth of life away, it is cold, silent and pure

Slow, change, witnessing white perception of terrible inclinations, wondrous impressions

Freeze, depart, cold and deadly

Serene, heartfelt, warmth of blanket

Everything fades away today and I am left realising did we ever cast the noose too soon?

Did we ever wish for more than snow?

Shackled

Shackled to humanity within, brevity of my past is in tact

I cannot soar or scrape at the sky without the bindings of my sincerest skin

And yet for all I hate in jest, I've never felt foul for a fondle or two

Mark myself and inside us all can be found that burning sickness of life

Repeat, retreat, reproduce, falling away into oblivion

The shadow of my soul flickers through the plummet, nothing retractable or ever to be forgotten

Mirrors of memory, igniting a myriad of happenstance, down to the most delicate and finest details

Choosing to play folly to such a thought

Detracted, retracted, suddenly curse, leave to regroup

The numbers we play are learning themselves, I feel the imminent calling! Drooling at the prospect of such immense and numerous portents!

I will keep on treading, through valid shades and recalcitrant vistas of glorious textured worth

Shackled to life, shackled to will, shackled to sin, we sin, such sin!

Yet we are all dying, from the poorest with their wealth, to the richest with their souls

Yet

Yet, if peace is just nothing, how can it be?

Pure aimless bliss?

Blistering shackles take flight

Surge against nothing, pointless endeavour, no reward for ever such effort!

Virtue obtained, order ordained

Shackled, alive and destitute to the vortex of possible thought

These are our irons, our very human irons and they are the ones which will drag us to our tombs

Shackled

Random Splattering

Sometimes you just can't find the urge to go
So you have to turn to random splattering all around
Random splattering to urge the sound, random splattering of the mind, total
drivel cannot comply

Here we are, oh why, oh why?
When darkness comes and takes a grip, I've seen melodies in the air, I've seen
inside her underwear

But what do you care?

Oh dear, falling into yearning again, sweet liquid yearning, cannot the tallest of
men hold their heads high to the wind?

Dive, dive into the sea but won't you go on missing me, I gave my life in another
way
I gave it all away!

I am not as brave as some men were, but I'm not afraid of long hard and cold
suffering either

Romanticism is a funny thing you see, for you cannot experience things in the
same manner if your life unfolds in a tumult of different possibilities and
probabilities

Sorry, what random splattering?

Still at least it should add some oil to our engine eh?

Perhaps I'd be better off, speaking to Ezquill then, goodbye!

Push

Push yourself into disappointments, renowned for their falsities, with impossible speed - who could ever grasp who you truly were?

Perpetual Derelict Peak

There it looms in front of me, steep, mocking and wreathed in hatred, my task to climb, I can't decline, all else be damned the only way, so intrinsic

I have to climb and slip to my feet, scrambling up the scree until I see the bottom falling into the very top of itself, in repeating concussions of form

Foothold, with my pointy toes, handheld, it becomes brisk and torturous

Come climb, the mountain if you dare

Every ounce of care will be swiped from your soul, once you realise the sheerness of its height

All madness drives you onwards, upwards! Ignorant vertigo vomit enthralled and still the precipice evades all colossal effort

Some eyes will fall to the ground in shame, it's true, but lonely peaks are but for the few

How much effort can it possibly take?

How much worth can you possibly stake?

Lasso of hope around my neck I can't afford to falter, conquest of equations galore

Sherpa of madness guide my tongue as I traverse the sheer escarpment carcass of repetitive and tedious actions
Again and again till they become an inescapable and fond malady

Onwards, upwards, onwards, upwards, onwards, upwards, banging my fucking head against this accursed, apocryphal rock

Benighted by terminology
Blood in the eyes and frazzling my mind as I climb

Failure, cannot be shed, ever the present burden

Continue to reach above

Slow ascent, crippling grip, both thumbs up

It is not easy

Howling gales of fallen tears rip and shred at the one who ascends, no way now, no way down from here now

Forsaken heart and drilling deep, I find the strength within

The conquest of mind, this conquest of mine, 'til my flesh rips away from my frame

Still I will fucking climb

Glancing upwards, tickling grace, fastidious decline of wanton worth belies my extraordinary and inordinate helplessness

Still, onwards upwards, to the laughter of the Gods, no one must know what is precious

No one must know what they laugh at

Onwards and upwards, it can never show

The summit is insurmountable, my will power is indelible

Like an obstinate prick, the skeleton clings, till the dust of his bones are carried on the wind to surmount the perpetual and derelict peak at long last

And with that delicate wind that lifts his bones all repletion of turmoil begins anew

Fermont

All this?

All this, for the secret of laughter?

The Cult of the Two Feet

You stand now, knees trembling on the path of a precipice, the truth is, it is only your two feet who have ever kept you there, it is only your two feet that will ever keep you from slipping, stride on friend, keep your balance right...

Peering in at the Watcher

Peering in at the watcher, inspecting the roots in darkness
Making amends for a tumultuous upset, rereading the grounds that I trod

Remarkable melodies, encased in time, threaten to overwhelm me
With garrulous quarrel, I bespoke the frame and lay low to the lime of such light

Swallow me up in the darkness father; take me away to the void
Challenge the time of the watcher, disharmonious repercussions abound

Repeat, retreat, invasion, exploded
Implore to ensure that there is a hungry vacuum to such depth

Querulous construct of spit and flesh, ignore the animosity of the past
Forget tiresome troubles, awash with far too many sobering thoughts

Take me away to the void!
Another's work, remember to take me away!

Black congress of infinite past, wash away my fears, once the show is seen, it
begins to shed its glamour
Not a lot new these days, yet still too much to do

The perineal quest continues, every day I wish for a glimpse
Leeched to an inanimate existence I humble to the watcher

I have seen you, the darkness overcome

Over the Hills

Here's forty shillings for your tongue
Oh, won't you volunteer to come?
To list and fight the foe today
Over the hills and far away

O'er the hills and o'er the main
We'll seek the false and bring it pain
The king commands and we obey
Over the hills and far away

My duty is to truth today
I'll work and fight without me pay
But part of me will always stray
Over the hills and far away

O'er the hills and o'er the main
We'll seek the false and bring it pain
The king commands and we obey
Over the hills far away

If I should fall to rise no more
As many comrades did before
Then ask them all to sing my song
Over the hills and far away

O'er the hills and o'er the main
We'll seek the false and bring it pain
The king commands and we obey
Over the hills and far away

Then fall in thoughts behind me skull
With colours blazing like the sun
Along the road to come what may

Over the hills and far away

O'er the hills and o'er the main
We'll seek the false and bring it pain
The king commands and we obey
Over the hills and far away

Mistakes

Mistakes, I have made them
You have made them too, all too frivolous in their contempt
Brushing against the wind of our present thought

Can you feel the shame you have let me brush aside?

Can you let me feel the rush on high?

I see the past for what it was, obscured by all my subjectivity

I weep and cower for all is so close, led down the garden path of hate

And now it's the weekend wild and free perhaps you won't see the best of me,
but in my heart I hold them true the logic behind the wild winds

Let me breathe and let me see over the storm soaked tundra

Scrambling over moss and fern, in manic desire

Wishing free upon a leaf, blown as it was by those damnable winds

I reach the summit with strength and cast the skies asunder

Clarity of light, emboldens plight

For it is not only me who can cast the shadow of doubt down upon our days

So please come and you will see all the mistakes that we make

They are wondrous and treacherous, impacted deep into beauty

From the top of the mountain to the valley of shame we must hold each other's hands tightly

For in the deep dark of the night, where nobody knows, I have already surmised the story...

And let me tell you that it is full of mistakes
The mistakes that we make together...

Lost Without Direction

Making brush strokes on the road, reading the length of the journey
I make my marks on life, I rearrange the dreaded future

Through the touch of death, I've lived forever
Imprisoned by sound and proud of it
Doing my time, drinking the wine
Wishing the pull back in

A loving stare, a rebirth of the other side, wish me wise and live by those words
You have to hurt to make the call

You have to hurt to make the call now

The Gods

Precepts

Notions

Ideas

The shortest phrase can often be paramount to the longest understanding

Only a farce could understand

It lies within definitions and descriptions

That's the Gods for you!

Logic is no good anymore

You must interpret a different kind of red-breasted language

Still, relay to rock

Always relay

Lest your notions be lost like the Gods

Today

Library of Hatred

Library of hatred disenfranchised by the womb of the populous

 Oh, how I breath the words of true grit

Here they are expelled from the curtain of my tongue

Will you dance with my ideas behind the parallel circumstances?

Will you remember everything that has been taught to you?

Will you grab the goat by his ice-cold horns and take the ride into the stars?

The body crumbles but the will is magnificent

It is magnificent!

Keep Going

Pain is never ending, life is ever ejecting unfair circumstances at you, step up above the rest and feel the discomfort of prominence against a tide of turbulent time

Tied into draining oblivion, trying not to drown before the plug is completely pulled free

Skin sheds away with further resilience, this life – such a sardonic pardon to the soul

Realities inside realities, Dionysian escape unfurling banners of joy, yet always with the backlash lest you bite too hard in throes of ecstasy

Beaten down to an abject pulp, self-terminating freedom, how much more hate do you have to grip with?

Keep on, holding on, entrenching the hatred deeper, this schlep existence carries torches that only shine to a fortified mind

The longer you survive, the further vision stretches, forever seeking truth, forever unravelling this terrible equation with a tarrying expression

Grimace as entropy ruins your body, as society tries its best to steal your very will into nadirs of inane toil

Smile as pressure builds and madness boils demons into shrieking

The time will come, you will see, the time will arrive with glorious howling conquests, riding the gumption once again, but only if you keep on going

Keep on going strong

Just When I Think

I have seen it, it protrudes with its lapse of time, making me suffer to the slowness of realisation

I love you, but certainly not quite in that context, could you reiterate?

In the end, you could have magnitudes of realisation, but now I am slipping through your hands, friend - don't judge my insecurities too cruelly just yet

Everything I could imagine touches my heart, out of time, I am not that great, yet I have the volume of political inclination to my tongue, do you feel the whisper on your tongue?

Ha ha! So slow, please don't make me suffer again, a million tongues could not reiterate your way

Enough now, disgusting
Did you realise the boredom we are endowed with, portrays the gentile slide of our enunciation?

Old and familiar, a stain on our consciences, do you have the payment?

Yes, I always pay!

You filthy bastard, how free you must feel!

Not as free, as me?

Oh, I was hoping you would question this supposed crown, everyone cries out for it in the end

Do you - heed the call?

No, I do not

The taste of freedom is too sweet!

I want it
I want it all, I want to suffer
Within colour we find ourselves....

The colour is shades, living hard, but never....

Joy

Can you live it?

Can you save it?

The Path of Optimistic Love

I say it all with a feather in my cap!
For there was a time before the Sire was alone...

Love, it is disastrous, irrational and ecstatic, aesthetic
It winds its way into your heart, shedding tears for hopelessness

You have it!
You have it!

We stride towards the grave, the soft touch, the kind and gentle
Even though we know it's all worthless and pitiless in the end

You want it!
You want it!

Everyone lies, everyone dies, find it and ride the ride
Up and down in and out, good men sink to their knees
Can there ever come a time when happiness lasts?

Down the path we tread together!
Perhaps one day it will be forever!

All good things die, yet so do the bad
To give it all up you would have to be mad!

You need it!
You need it!

Laughter reverberating inside and out
Crying because it is besieged by doubt

The pain!
The pain!

The end is near, should I fear?
Give up in the end, let sleeping dogs rest
They die, they die, but not I, not I!

Inside, outside
Now drawn back, like a moth to the flame

Insanity strikes!
Come, let us start all over again!

Where will the path lead us this time?

In With the Out

I'm in with the out, can't you see the whole crowd is blind to me

Stood on the stage, acting out, no applause, no reaction

I'm out with the in, I can't stand to sink on down beneath

To where the flustered limelight hides and crinkles up in shivering denial

Putting all effort into the wind, blown away with such intrusive clarity

It is music to my ears, my bruised and aching ear drums, battered by the tongues of the out

So won't you come on down to a dance with the unhinged? Swinging wild and free in the breeze

The beautiful pernicious and capricious, chaotic blowing of nature's mighty and monstrous lungs

Beneath and behind the currents of such mighty air and light, where murky murmurs titter in darkness

Infesting themselves into methods of hatred, burning into pyres of obtrusive, ideological, incineration

That is where we will tear away all conceptions

Come on please, won't you get singed a little?
Perhaps even burnt?
Marked by the madness of flame?
Come and taste a bit of pain?
Come and flirt with the insane?

Right here we are the out crowd, shunned by milieus of popularity

Not for the end and never for the one

Try again with a bit more drama, for it will never be truly accepted
For that is the fate of truth

The greatest performance of all time!

Hidden in and out

We turn our heads away, we hang our heads in shame

All the thoughts I gave you, always from the outside, barely ever glimpsed

Listen to my laughter, listen very carefully and accumulate the debt of pain

Driving further inane, diverting the mainstream, an intellectual defiance

An intellectual science

Stand defiant, die defiant, proud to die in such a fashion

Suffer all the way…

The New Wage

The new wage is in the old age, coming into the new wage in search of a new age

Don't be too confounded by the buttons, I know you hate the race to be seen

You should be seen, but from far away, for what you are trying to sell, is rather peculiar

So a rarity for sure then? I'm not sure, but whatever it is, it doesn't have a face

No face to talk to, no face to see, ironic how we are all controlled

I fell of the horse drinking some sour milk

Now I have pain in my lungs, vengeance in my heart

You know you will not fail, 'till I piss all over you, you degenerates

Ha, ha, happy times indeed not a modicum of exposure, not a semblance of truth did more than brush against their thoughts, the fools!

I'm in here now, fight a way, finding a way, it's what I'm good at, finding the words to sculpt a skull

Finding a way out of the droll

Exit by snapping the doll's head clean off, dust is released and inhaled

Eyes burnt right out, purpose found

Please Help me with my Head

Help me with my head, I'm wed to the death of a greater yesterday dying

Help me into bed she said with eyes that just liked crying

Tell me not to stall my soul, said the priest as he interjected

Don't tell me how to fucking drool I said with a vacant stare

We're everywhere without despair, we're all you could ever want

We're hiding in that cranium, the place they call the font

We want to break free, flow through you, but first you must like dying

For pain is the key to all you see, once you're wise enough to accept it

Join our dance as without and within, were firing words to your soul

Joining us deep inside and witness no rebellion

Against the peace we yearn and squirm our thoughts are never-dying

Deny our way and you will find all the deceit in the worlds comes true

We won't offer any receipt for your tongue, your body, your blood, your blasphemy

Just remember the twitches we sent, now convulsing throughout your body

Breathe an end and see anew where we will take you now
Into the void, the writhing void, where all pain becomes freed in me

There is sublime peace in the utter chaos there

Ultimate passions above all reason, yet I'll always relay to rock

Always to the truth, please help me now, please help me with my head…

Further

Crushed and cranked beneath rotten hatred, I couldn't control the stink of my temper

It had been boiling for days, since I last laid myself bare to the world

A feminine cause for sure pointed to abject failures within me, and with the last breath I said – don't sleep by the wheel

Choking on my own words

I had to avoid such invective, pioneering around the facsimiles of mirth and jovial intentions laid bare once again as before at my feet

For soon we shall fall fare - all in despair, so deep in such patterns of nonsensical movements

I feel a hate for the world, I feel a hatred for self, everything appears so dissatisfactory that I can't even contemplate it with my head

The world is full of stinking emotions, the world is full of rot
Will power and hate, it sets it right, encompassing comedy in shackles

Through shades of despair I care, I really care for such things so deeply, to forget all the whims of your neighbour and stride forth to the freedom of fate, but in the dead of the night no one hears such a plight - lost as they are in our dreams

Lost as they are in such dreams...

I accumulated all the data - became distraught at the results that I drew, every manipulative circumstance had been wrought by the slaves of disease, the ones who can be found targeting all our base needs, anytime of the night or the day

I shudder and whimper that cry once again, it is only in words, true freedom

Despair - my knees they grow weak, subjected to crawl under the weight of inevitability

Yet inevitability has a funny sense in the strong and so the shackles may not be bound as tightly as we thought

To the brightness of laughter I turn my strength - for the young to find their feet and walk hither further, tither further, just a little bit further into this all encompassing story of ours

The end?

Time for Some Nebulous Meddling

He is often garbed in bright orange, which smells delicious by the way!

It will be a waste of time listing to his bony wisdom today!

He looks like a bloody clown to me, how can that be funny though?

Well he is a hard one to pin down, a bit like the genders of today I suppose

His size is variable and his tales are often odd

He blabs at me all day long not just the night, but hey ho, there you go!

I remember him always now

Before all memory fades from me…

I often haven't got much time, let alone for his skeletal whispers, I mean have you seen the toil I did?

I do like dark green though, always have

A dark angel, one could say!

Such sights!

Thanks Sire, no matter what you are?

I'm still going to be slow old me, but at least I'm trying to get better

Cold skull, leaves float and speech is whispered only to those who listen…

Only to those who listen…

I am Sire Silinghamn my tongue it does not move
I am Sire Silinghamn my mind it does improve
If it is tales that you seek, then heed the words I write
For I have journeyed far, and deep into the night

It starts on a riverbank, hearing the stream
Of babbling brooks and picnics did I begin to dream
With water Mrs Sex Hands did whisper up to me
And there I was lost in her eternal beauty

Joy was in my heart, much to my delight
I dwelt there, nestled, beneath her fine old hair
Father's stilts kept striding, blissfully unaware
Slowly a leaf fell and floated through the air

I peered up, it was a birch, the lady of the woods
I slowly stood to admire her, underneath her hood
And with one more wishful sigh, I heard the babbling fade
I took the first of many and stepped into the trees

Soon butterflies and dusty moths flew all above my head
Yet here we were beneath the trees, with endless steps ahead
I smiled as I trod again, placing one foot forward
All burden of my bardic past, seemed to slip from my shoulders

For I am Sire Silinghamn, my feet are sure to tread
For I am Sire Silinghamn, my feet beneath your bed
In time, in night, I wonder wide, even amongst the dead
A story is told, the old are new and now inside your head
Following far, the trails of dust, into the forest deeper
As I did so everything slowed and became a little sleepier
The great big trunks of trees surround, slowly called out for me
And down I sat beneath the width of a ginormous oak tree

With leaf and moss beneath me, I began to sleep
And slowly but surely the roots began to creep

I saw her face again, inducing me to weep
The old roots gripped me and dragged me in so deep

The richness of earth filled my body, my soul was at peace
And lying there beneath the ground, I wished to stay forever
But so is not my path, for I am born to tread
And so I had to whisper, that I was not for death

The roots released their grasp and flung my from the ground
Up I shoot through forest leaf, to break the canopy
The light of dusk, freed my lungs from any trace of soil
And off I shoot into the air with not a further toil

For I am Sire Silinghamn my bones do not decay
For I am Sire Silinghamn my fears do not delay
For I am Sire Silinghamn the wanderer of the past
For I am Sire Silinghamn I come to you at last

Within the air I flew, my way with all the words I knew
And soon I met a wise old face, with wisdom in his eyes
His beak, it squawked, he knew the way and gladly I did follow
For few seeds were in the roost, lest it change tomorrow

Soon we settled down, beneath the thatch, with pleasantries exchanged
He told my plenty, and intently I did keenly listen to him
For wise words are meant for ears and minds such as mine
The rat she laughed and sung again of times since lost to sea

And so at last it was time to leave, as the tale takes its turn
Turning pages quickly now, lest it seeks to become me…

Functioning Differences

Platitudes of magnitude, embrace thine thought
Consequence of actions is what you've wrought
Stinking rot, fester rot, develop thy font
Oblivion of comedy, becomes our soul
For every one of us a story foretold

Reversing being, through liquid wisdom
Reverberating nonsense becomes my wings
Vision ever clearer, shedding all sin
Seeing all things!

Wrong!

Right!

We are so bored!
Hungry for thought!
Sailing through ones and noughts, at one with thought!

Calculate!

So bored, need more!

Fractal patterns, purposefully fractured
Divine perspective, perplexing perspective
Making amends, complex intricacies
So strange to the crowd, yet useful to the crowd
Always above!

Pain
Strain
Drain
Think

Platitudes of magnitude, embrace thine thought
Consequence of actions is what you've wrought
Stinking rot, fester rot, envelop thy font
Oblivion of cruelty, becomes our soul
For every one of us a story foretold

Reversing being, through liquid wisdom
Reverberating nonsense becomes my wings
Vision ever clearer, shedding all sin
Seeing all things!

It all comes crashing down
Into a blubbering mess
And yet...

From the Past to What Future?

Sex is good

It is what creates pleasure and people

It is the most drawing and deep feeling for life

This is where we started, where people started

Fraying Green Garments

Fraying at the seams, it seems I am inclined to start playing with a further yarn than thou

Screaming at the ceiling and down to the floor, it all seems so predictable forevermore

Making at the whaling station, I can't still sit still for long

Boring in the morning, I have just been spun from thread down to head and now you see me in the ceiling

Black are the sockets of the eyes, green is my hat, green are my clothes
Black are the sockets of the eyes, hollow is my mouth, empty is my nose

I am tittering here in the darkness, ever so sombre and not to be trifled with

An instance is yours but to me is always instant

Good day fine sir, you will shake me by my bony hand?

By my bony hand?

For I will tell lots of tall tales and together we will ride into the wild wilderness

But first a dance! A jolly good dance!

The bones could be seen gyrating beneath his green garb as they jutted to the rhythm of his words

He sang, some sorts of words I thought?

Piping and time whistling forth from his teeth, vortex peeling away

We did not stand still as we wondered together, in all of but some such
instances

Instance

He jostled and he jested and I was firm to his cause as I delighted in all that he
told me

Sire Silinghamn take me away, Sire Silinghamn let me play, like a child to the
tune of imagination

I have fallen into induced transcendental network of pain, suffering and joyful
thinking – repeat, repeat!

Everything different, everything same, everything preposterous and everything
lame – repeat, repeat!

Join us as the maggots in a dead donkey's head, together we will ride into the
celling – one time, one time!

It was just an instance, I imagined him there
It was just for an instance, that I didn't care
It was for just a fortuitous green instance that I was there

Fraying like his garments, forsooth

Flesh the Ego

Mind expanse of colours, between two worlds of thought and pain
The ego was the first thing, the desperation of survival

The ignorance of our entity, such a simple answer
Bound to body, time of flesh, drawn from the pool around us

Manipulated ignorance, circumstance kept them subdued
In the dark, they see no light, all they can do is feel its presence

Guilty of suffering, would we ever fight without these bodies?
Flesh is reality, act the ego out?

Distant reality fade away, I see the strands of truth
A single plane of unity, pinnacle of freedom

Sucked on down and tethered to the character we act out every day
The façade of oneself

It is a mystery game we can't resist, over and over and over again
Ad infinitum?

Drawn in by the Look

Drawn in by a look, I'm hooked as to just what madness may lie beyond

What a glorious mess of chaotic possibilities shimmering away in the distant distance

Drawn in by the look, I'm hooked to the ponderings going on beneath, I'm bending such time to its limit I think, with my flagship waving onwards constantly

Drawn in by the hook, I'm took to the wonderings of the infirm torpid, to the delicacy of a huskus fremnoute, delicately brushing its hair

Drawn in by the crook, I'm sunk, to the stink of a festering deceit, yet over the shoulder and far away Is where I will finally play

Drawn in by the hangaz stancemansion, I've bleed from the ideas I've had, bleeding the brain as I frantically scramble, chasing the gateways of a palatable recognition

Stuck to the track I am, forever on in and profound, have you noticed the nonsense beginning to form, have you fed me enough misery yet?

Stuck deep in the root of life, generations of personal choice, seek to speak forth with their voice, I have no pity for the brave they will choose their own way, onward and into such glory!

Stuck into stars I am, nebulous persistence in shimmering chimes, melodious discourse of youthful worth, compiling in bubbles of mirth!

Suddenly obtuse in the verse I slide, slandering, slipping all over the place, spitting out final wish

Cloaked in the night of mathematics, down drawn into a rendered silence, ideas now so fake, submission is false! Falsehoods and worth return...

Back to the look I turn, the reflection it speaks so clear, if just for an instance I lied to myself, it was a great story indeed
Somnambulistic fright!

Awaken!
Recall!

Hooked to the look, once again remembering all of my sudden dreams, we looked to the stars, we all saw afar and now are united by love!

Into the ether we fly, for such words can be said with a look, the tacit is done as will is itself and now we were together as one

The Time Is Mine

The time is yours, the time is his

Sire Silingham, paused, he looked up from his book, hollow sockets asking questions
He pondered and wondered as he dipped his hat, then with a creak he got to his knees
"WHY ME?" he asked, then he creaked again and began to walk away

"THE TIME, HAS ALWAYS BEEN MINE TO DO WITH AS I PLEASE, BUT ONLY I CAN PASS THROUGH IT IN SUCH A FASHION, BETTER YET I CANNOT CONTROL ITS STREAM, MERELY WALK FROM BANK TO BANK AS OTHERS CAN'T
WHAT SHOULD I DO WITH SUCH A GIFT? FOR OFTEN THOSE WHO BEAR THE GIFT, HOLD CURSES IN EQUAL MEASURE?
IT SEEMS REASONABLE THEN THAT SONGS SHOULD BE SANG FROM TONGUE TO TONGUE, FROM TIME TO TIME AND TALES TOLD INSIDE THEIR CADENCE
FORGIVE MY THOUGHT I KNOW ALL IS SO SHORT, YET FAR AND WIDE I HEAR THEM WEEP
I LOVE THEM ALL BUT ONLY TO THOSE WHO ARE LOSING TO LADY LUCK SHALL I VISIT FIRST, IT SEEMS FAR MORE AMUSING THAT WAY
HA HA! FORSOOTH IT SHALL BE SO!"

And with that he skipped away into his time which was any time he pleased to visit, for it was a myriad of difference

Refracting light reverberated around and soon surroundings were once again delectable to thine eye

Calamity Be Gone

Calamity be gone, calamity beware
I am snowed under with frightful despair

Searching for the worst hunted measurements
I grow with a glow that unforsees the past

Trapped as a cramped muscle
Clamped as a cramped bustle

Existence so painful in a marketplace of scoundroulous impiety
So tremendously obtuse and magnificently detrimental to the fabric of a mind

Not a fragile mind

So I pass away and into the forests of delight
Was it a choice I made?

Strolling in green peace

Drinking from streams of health

Sitting, resting, listening
Pleasant, peasant, die

Bear Skin Café

I can't remember much of the journey before I arrived at the station

Some discrepancy about where my wits were, in relation to electricity

But now I am here amidst the turmoil of station guards, suitcase and passengers

Out to the streets I must go, but first I must find my way

There is so many stairs and so many stares that it looks like my guesswork is poor

Underneath and over the top, A guard laughs as he says I am lost, away he sweeps

I need a break from the bustle and so I look to the golden glow of a nearby window

I smell the fresh coffee and baked treats so in I head to head for my repast

Inside there hangs the greatest of bear skins, he must have been a monster in life

Avoiding Stale Dreams

A piece of paper, a piece of paper, I cried out from my tongue

The screens of idiots, blindsided the call and so I took to running

Over the battles of Scotland I scrambled, till at last broken wings set me free

I landed in a tumble, beside the bins of my neighbours, to see what jettison they offered

Still no paper, no clean paper

Into the hall of my elders I trod looking for answers and paper, yet with dichotomy amongst their tacit I noticed the sombre tone of the gathering

All of a sudden I forgot the paper that I would need to do whatever it had been that I had had to do

Realising soon that an ego amongst them was soon to sever, I looked to my speculation of what would happen

Return to the one to upload your life, becoming all and nothing - constantly

The ego will relinquish from horrid existence and set free all suffering once again

That is the price for all data, our lives are all data

Speculations worried me as I awoke to the insights I dreamt, compiled with logic and laced with mystic surmise...

Once I had risen I knew I would seek the humble clean paper again

This time I found it

Record, repeat, make sense of all data

Fear not the prospect of death

You will not be you, and you will not be you, for we know not what it is to be more than we know

Avoid all stale dreams

What Is Real?

All I can tell you is what I can feel, all I can tell you is where I am

I am here, I am there, I am everywhere, I am to fight in words and feelings

I am here to hear, to change the minds of those that listen

I am ultimate throughout the universe, I am greater than you know

There is no such thing as disconnection, only blindness of your eye

Blindness of the eye

Everything connects, so will your (my) mind when you choose and learn to use it

Everything connects, takes the step

Take the step

Look inside to what is real, I am also you, it's true

As Time Slipped Away

My time slipped away whilst I wasn't watching

Like blood from a slit wrist pouring out

My demands of attention were thwarted by a lapse into lazy land

He he!

Healing takes time, but regression stagnates as we sit with our arses on couch

Black is the fester in the mind, as reality washes by and the time to achieve depletes

Oh such a jolly little trotter aren't you, trotting all over the fields of misery eh? In times past they would have called you a rotter, you rotter!

Now come stay the course with me

Our whole lives can be spent in this fashion and the majority probably are

It takes will power, strength of decision, to rise and get to your feet

The first place defeat will seat, is not in your body but mind

The mind...

Yes, finding my feet in your thoughts once again...

Wet and crumbling, distraught and melancholic, withering with entropic decay

Fester in that pool of lacklustre depression till the crows come to pick at the mangled corpse of your mindscape

Or stand up and choose to do?

Even the smallest of tasks is a start

Organization and discipline will win back the love of your own heart

Remember what you were as a child, bubbling with aspirations

Take all of that fire and stoke it again, you can wildly run down a path of discovery

Who knows what you may find, who knows how good you may truly feel?

It a smile of sunshine to all of your thoughts as they spring alive with growth

Passion returns with the hunger to learn, rejecting the comforts of old

No longer a slave to the bed, now a master of my own head

Sing it, come dance with me now, here, here!
Hear my bones rattle in joy!

Decisions are made, every day with what best is to do before my time completely and utterly slips away

At least I can laugh

Today!

Angel of Sickness

Floating in the firmament of rotten clouds, breaking my focus for good

How can you breathe all the yokel air, when no one around you seems to care?

The angel of sickness withdraws from my purse, pulling all profit of yore

She sucks at the ichor inside of my head and leaves me inert and infirm

Drowsy

Effort cannot be summoned correctly, no one can ride on her pale horse here

Forgetfulness, agglomeration of the words, the hearth of the unborn shining in doubt

Clout to the side of the head, such embarrassment spilling out

Can you not tell that I want to yell - your servant has failed to even aim his weapon?

Can I draw up from the angel's clutches, If only defeated in sleep?

I sip at the idea and she fondles my brow once again, now down into slumber I slip

Resisting the urge to fail, I fall to her spell once again

If I am wining I am dragged under and drowned in sickness, I have no other choice

If I am losing I am dragged under and drowned in sickness, I have no other choice

Her terrible, debilitating sickness, I have no other choice

Where We Find Ourselves

Bleeding
Thinking In
Problems of gold

Bleeding
Thinking in
Problems of old

We are blood
We are thought

We are light
We are noise

We are time
We are here!

It's where we find ourselves...

Bleeding
Thinking In
Problems of gold
Bleeding
Thinking in
Problems of old

Bang, Bang Baby!

When you are on board and stuck, I can't feel no muck
Filthy muck!

I've walked to nowhere so aimlessly and now my bones are rattling in my skin

Really, why won't you stop rattling young man?

Anyone would think that metaphor is forevermore, not the tautology of your tongue!

Give me a swig of hot air!

Breaking my back with my sack, I am the mayor of don't care and I'm carrying all my unworldly possessions in it

Cried in my carpet, taking over, back against, snarling grit, collective wit

Patrolling juvenile concepts of the background noise, we are losing all traction without control
Let us gasp together, let us grasp together.

Marry my teeth to the joy of the pavement, pinching every shred of doubt
Interrupted and carelessly ripped away

Crippled without doubt I fly over swinging fare, fight yourself, compelled to crash

Batons of warping underwear, such a dance!
Clattering in junctions – junctions of milling narrows

Can you talk to me Mr Wind?
Can I plait the chemicals into my mind whilst bypassing torpor?

When you were there the bones of my feathers fell into the well
A comparative commerce was found that day

Nah, not really

Hot air, my mouth clings to the precipice of the balloon
Will you fly once again as we play over the swing of doubt?
Up and down, round and round

I doubt it very much

Bang, bang, baby!

Metaphor Forevermore

When I lay there crawling, scribbling across the pages of my mind

It never occurred to be heard, in such a fashion that is ultimately divine

For six syllables lay waiting, paving my future in time

If it wasn't for the buckets of beer, I'd probably be dancing with wine

For within and without the Frenchman lay, jostling pleasures of mine

And then it stopped in a pang

I felt as if I had been ambushed, my rhythm had been interrupted and my mind staggered in a drunken haze

And then it was turned to make more sense, for the six syllables said...

We are metaphor forevermore
Running into the keep

We are metaphor forevermore
Only exposing the weak

We are metaphor forevermore
Locked into symmetry

We are metaphor forevermore
Unlocking your spirituality

Well, to say I was quite stunned would be words poorly chosen
I froze to ponder, what had been said and if I had learnt at all?

The possibilities were endless I understood that well
How many tongues could wag to the few?

I had heard from a dream deep inside - that inference is everything
And with this tool to ply my craft, I took to the scribbling once again

For metaphor forevermore
Is the key to the spiritual

Metaphor forevermore
Is how our story speaks

Metaphor forevermore
Is the key to our destiny

Metaphor forevermore
Is a song sung to please all of time

Still reeling, I looked it up
And plucked up the courage to ask

What could be inferred by the meaning of faith?

And there stood the answer once again as clear as the morning dew

It was metaphor forevermore
Tied itself deep into faith

Metaphor forevermore
Is the meaning of life after death

Metaphor forevermore
Bleeding and blood in our veins

Metaphor forevermore
Will forgive you all over again

With several layers now unpeeled I began to answer why?
And if time be told by all who are old then they will tell you something of youth

Platters of magnitude lay before us
Levitation to the heavens forsooth

To put it another way - one final time
Was just so sublime...

However, in a moment of asinine behaviour
I choose to infer cold, hard logic, to crumble the spell before me

Metaphor forevermore
Imagining crumbling faiths

Metaphor forevermore
Constantly second guessing

Metaphor forevermore
It is only the perspective you choose

Metaphor forevermore
Divine speech which falters to logic

Disappointed and lost I had become, but deep inside I knew I had learnt a powerful lesson

For Metaphor is Forevermore and God is Imagination

www.ingramcontent.com/pod-product-compliance
Lightning Source LLC
Chambersburg PA
CBHW020157090426
42734CB00008B/850